"There are books that calm our anxious souls, b[...] of practical wisdom, and books that re-anchor [...] truths. This book does all three—and it does so [...] you're a parent, especially one with a teen, these pages are jesu[...] gift to you."

—**Chad Bird, author of several books, including**
Your God Is Too Glorious

"Wise, clearheaded, and gospel-focused—Jessica Thompson has done us all a great service by providing answers for how to help our children experience real peace in a world where fear and anxiety are being stirred up every day. There is real hope here."

—**Bob Lepine, cohost of** *FamilyLife Today*

"As a mama who will parent four teenagers in this lifetime, I appreciate the wisdom on the subject of anxiety that Jessica brings to this book. Every page is soaked in humor, real-life examples, and eye-opening ideas about what anxiety looks like for today's teenagers, all while pointing us back to our God, who loves us and asks us to cast our anxieties on Him."

—**Jamie Ivey, host of** *The Happy Hour with Jamie Ivey* **podcast**
and author of *If You Only Knew*

"*How to Help Your Anxious Teen* is the unfussy parenting guide I didn't know I needed. With her signature blend of grace and humor, Jessica Thompson shakes us awake, urging us to pay attention and ask the hard questions. Fear and inadequacy wither as we lean on the unshakeable goodness of God through it all. What a relief! I'll return to this one again and again."

—**Shannan Martin, author of** *The Ministry of Ordinary Places*
and *Falling Free*

"If you are parenting an anxious child, Jessica's gospel-centered perspective is just what you need! Jessica equips us with a preventative and pressure-free approach to ensure we don't become another source of anxiety in our teens' already pressure-filled lives. And best of all, Jessica continually points us to the power of God's Word and the hope we have in Jesus."

—**Jeannie Cunnion, author of** *Mom Set Free*

HOW TO HELP YOUR *Anxious Teen*

Jessica Thompson

HARVEST HOUSE PUBLISHERS
EUGENE, OREGON

Cover design by Bryce Williamson

Cover photo © hannahgleg / Getty Images

Published in association with Wolgemuth & Associates, Inc.

How to Help Your Anxious Teen
Copyright © 2019 by Jessica Thompson
Published by Harvest House Publishers
Eugene, Oregon 97408
www.harvesthousepublishers.com

ISBN 978-0-7369-7671-8 (pbk.)
ISBN 978-0-7369-7672-5 (eBook)

Library of Congress Cataloging-in-Publication Data

Names: Thompson, Jessica, 1975- author.
Title: How to help your anxious teen / Jessica Thompson.
Description: Eugene, Oregon : Harvest House Publishers, [2019] | Includes
    bibliographical references.
Identifiers: LCCN 2019000379 (print) | LCCN 2019003549 (ebook) | ISBN
    9780736976725 (ebook) | ISBN 9780736976718 (pbk.)
Subjects: LCSH: Parenting—Religious aspects—Christianity. | Parent and
    teenager—Religious aspects—Christianity. | Anxiety in adolescence.
Classification: LCC BV4529 (ebook) | LCC BV4529 .T554 2019 (print) | DDC
    248.8/45—dc23
LC record available at https://lccn.loc.gov/2019000379

Printed in the United States of America

    19 20 21 22 23 24 25 26 27 / BP-AR / 10 9 8 7 6 5 4 3 2 1

Contents

1

The Problem

The sound of the espresso machine made it hard to hear her timid voice. I had to lean forward and strain to catch what she said. She fiddled with her paper coffee cup and repeatedly crushed the crumbs of her muffin with her thumb.

"I am so anxious all the time. I don't know what to do. My friends all told me that cutting helped them deal with it. So I tried it. I don't know if it helps or not, but it did get my mind off all the things I was worried about."

I put my hand on her arm and noticed it was littered with little nicks, some fresher than others, some scarred over. My heart hurt for her. She was only 14, but she felt the crushing weight of anxiety every single day. Her body exposed the internal conflict she tried to hide. She was worried about school, church, her family, and boys. She had experienced an incredibly tough year, and things didn't seem to be looking up for her.

Her story is not exceptional in any way. I have a 19-year-old son, a 17-year-old son, and a 14-year-old daughter, and all three of them have told me that they experience anxiety at some level or another. Teenagers today are suffering from anxiety at increasingly alarming rates. Catch a teenager in a talkative mood, and they will tell you most of their friends are anxious. Anxiety has replaced depression as the number one problem teenagers deal with. From 2010 to 2017, anxiety has been the main reason kids seek mental health services, and each year has seen an increase in the number of teens seeking help. "This year, 51 percent of students who visited a counseling center reported having anxiety, followed by depression (41 percent), relationship concerns (34 percent) and suicidal ideation (20.5 percent). Many students reported experiencing multiple conditions at once."[1] The number of teenagers that have been admitted for attempted suicide has doubled over the last ten years.[2] This rate reaches its zenith when kids return to school each fall.

Anxiety feels like a weight. It has been described as the feeling of tripping—the "moment where you don't know whether you are going to catch yourself is how you feel all day long." Or "when you tap your pocket to get your wallet, and it is not there. You feel that every moment of every day." Or...

> like when you see cop lights in your rearview and you know you did something worthy to get a ticket. Coming down from an attack is like the cop flying past you, heart still racing, kinda shaky, sweaty, and it's all in the back of your head the rest of the day. You think how great it was that you didn't get pulled over this time, but you are painfully aware you might not get this lucky next time.[3]

According to the National Institution of Mental Health, anxiety is now the most common mental health disorder in the United States. Almost one-third of both kids and adults are affected by it.[4] Part of the problem of anxiety with our youth is that most of us adults view it as a part of everyday life—it's not a big deal, we tell them. This feeds into their anxiety; they don't believe we are taking them seriously, which in turn makes them more anxious.

I have always thought we should be most concerned with our children suffering from depression, but things are changing—anxiety is what we now should be looking out for.

It's important to understand that anxiety and depression often occur in the same teenager, and may need to be treated as two separate disorders. Anxiety is more likely to occur without depression than depression without anxiety. It may be that depression leads to anxiety—the negative state of mind of a depressed teenager lends itself to uncertainty. If you're not feeling good about yourself, or confident, or secure, or safe, anxiety may find fertile ground. It may also be because the regions of the brain affected by anxiety and depression are close together, and mutually affected.[5]

According to the *Diagnostic and Statistical Manual of Mental Disorders* (*DSM-5*),

> Fear is the emotional response to real or perceived threat, whereas anxiety is anticipation of future threat. Obviously, these two states overlap, but they also differ, with fear more often associated with surges of autonomic arousal necessary for fight or flight, thoughts of immediate danger, and escape behaviors, and anxiety more often associated with muscle tension and vigilance in preparation for future danger and cautious or avoidant behaviors.[6]

Or to put it more plainly, "Anxiety is the overestimation of danger and the underestimation of our ability to cope."[7]

The problem is real, and it doesn't seem to be going away. How do we help our children deal with it? Is the rise of anxiety in children real, or are they just identifying as anxious because they don't know how to cope with everyday stress? How does the good news of the life, death, resurrection, and ascension of Christ impact our anxious hearts? Questions abound. We need solid biblical answers and gospel truth to inform this part of our lives.

If you are a parent, youth worker, pastor, teacher, or mentor of teens, you know exactly what I am talking about—you see it every day: the rise of self-mutilation; the use of marijuana, vaping, or more serious drugs to help decrease unwanted feelings; the addiction to social media to escape the real world; the heightened reports of sleeplessness among teenagers.

In this book, we will start by looking outward—we will analyze the way society contributes to our teens' anxiety. This might be an easy cause-and-effect relationship to understand. The world provides lots of reasons to be anxious: social media, the lack of human interaction caused by social media and new technology, bullying, the temperament of the country...and those are certainly contributing to teenagers' anxiety. With the dawn of social media, teenagers have a different set of problems to deal with than we did when we were young. But society isn't the only place teenagers are facing pressure; they face similar stresses at home and in church.

After looking outward at society, we will turn our gaze inward and analyze the ways the church contributes to teens' anxiety. Despite the church's good intentions, the pressures to be a "good" Christian and "do big things for God" are driving our kids into despair and anxiety.

Then we will take a long, hard look in the mirror and see where we, as parents and caregivers, have contributed to the problem. Even though we want to help our kids, we may very well be one of the causative factors to their anxiety.

Lastly, we will look at how teens' broken thinking feeds their own anxiety. My prayer is that by the end of this book, you will be able to understand why they feel anxious and be better equipped to help them fight that feeling. Along the way, you may even learn a little about yourself and what causes you anxiety. But my deepest desire is that you walk away from this book grateful for Jesus's love. Grateful for the one who understands our anxious hearts and tells us not to fear. Grateful not only that we and our teens are forgiven for not trusting him but also that we stand perfectly righteous in his sight. When he looks at us, he sees the perfect record of Jesus Christ, who didn't once give in to the temptation of fear but always trusted his heavenly Father.

As a note, I write from a middle-class, female, white perspective, so my societal norms might be different from what you experience. Studies indicate that females are more likely to experience anxiety (approximately a two-to-one ratio),[8] and white Americans are more likely to be diagnosed with generalized anxiety disorder.[9] "The differences were significant: 8.6 percent of White Americans will experience symptoms of generalized anxiety disorder in their lifetimes, compared to just 5.8 percent of Hispanics, 4.9 of Black Americans, and 2.4 of Asian Americans."[10] I do think that although some societal norms may differ according to socioeconomic status, gender, and race, the human heart remains the same, and my prayer is that these chapters will be helpful no matter how we differ.

My guess is that if you picked up this book, you may very well be in the middle of a crisis. If that is the case, look over the chapters and see what might be most beneficial to you right now and start with that chapter—don't feel guilty about skipping around. And please, before you go any further, take a moment and pray. Pray that the Holy Spirit opens your eyes to see things that you haven't before. Pray that you don't feel overwhelmed or anxious as you look at and deal with this problem. Pray that you know that God is next to you in all this, that the Holy Spirit will guide and lead you, and that Jesus himself is praying for you and understands every temptation you may be experiencing. Pray that you don't look at your teen as a problem to be fixed but as a soul to be loved.

2

Mental Illness or Elevated Anxiety?

Before we get any further in the book, we need to make an important distinction. Let's begin with an illustration.

Recently, I was at a park with some friends when I overheard two dads talking. A little boy was clinging to one man's leg. It was clear that the child loved the parent and the parent loved the child. The dad's hand rested on the boy's back. The two men were talking about overrated quarterbacks, and then the subject switched to the beginning of the school year.

The dad with the son sighed heavily and started talking about how his son—I am assuming the one who was holding on to his leg as if it were a life preserver—was feeling anxious about starting kindergarten. The other dad listened as the man went on and on about how ridiculous it was for his boy to be anxious. I could almost see the boy shrinking as the dad went on to talk about how the boy was always with his mom and how that must be the problem. The boy needed to "man up." Yes, those were the dad's words.

Now, I assume that by saying the boy needed to "man up," the dad meant the son needed to go to school regardless of his feelings. But the dad's tone of voice and belittling words were difficult to hear. I don't know their situation at all or the struggles they might have had at home, but I could see the little boy's face fall as he heard his dad talk.

I wonder...was the boy really anxious, or was he just feeling the *normal* stress of starting something new with people he didn't know in a space he wasn't used to? Perhaps this young boy was experiencing a mental illness and clinical anxiety. Or maybe he was simply fearful of something new. No one would ever know because he was shut down before he even spoke.

The distinction lies between what is mental illness and what is elevated anxiety. Either way, if your teenager comes to you and tells you they are experiencing anxiety, you must take them seriously. Many parents or caregivers downplay their children's problems so they feel more in control of the situation. Do not give in to this temptation. In my own life, much to my shame, I have fallen into this habit—if I can just make my child see that their feelings are unreasonable, I think to myself, then all will be fine and life will go back to normal.

In the story I relayed earlier, I saw a little bit of my own interactions with my daughter. When she expressed feelings of sadness in the past, I told her she just needed to go for a walk outside. Now it is a joke between us, but it wasn't a laughing matter at first. She pointed out that when I said that to her, it made her even sadder than how she felt before she spoke to me; she knew I was blowing her off. Regardless of whether my advice was sound, it wasn't what she needed. She needed me to stop and listen, not ignore her feelings and move on. The suppression of your children's feelings will have the exact opposite effect from what you desire.

The Beach Ball

I have often heard anxiety described as a big beach ball that you try to push under the water. Do you remember playing that game as a child? *Keep that beach ball under the water as long as you can!* You would spend all your energy keeping that ball below the water level. Finally, when you couldn't hold it anymore, it would pop to the surface with such great force, it would shoot into the air! Laughing, giggling, and screaming would ensue.

Our kids are working at keeping the beach ball—their anxiety—under the water. They are trying to keep their thoughts in control and push down their negative feelings. When they confess their anxious thoughts to us, often our advice is to push down harder. When all their energy is exhausted and they can't keep their anxious thoughts at bay anymore, they shoot up to the surface, just like the beach ball but in a very dramatic way.

Their outburst of emotion is inconvenient and interrupts our routine, but don't forget the prayer we closed out the last chapter with: We prayed we would see our children as image bearers and souls to be loved, not problems to be solved. So when that beach ball shoots straight up and gets you all wet, remember what exactly it is you are dealing with. This person is not an inconvenience. They are not a project. They are an image bearer, a soul just like your own, with thoughts and emotions and desires—they are your loved one.

Atmosphere of Grace

Hopefully, you have created an atmosphere of grace in your home, where your child feels comfortable opening up their life and emotions to you. If you don't know if you have that with your child or if you fear you don't, why not ask them? Ask them if they feel comfortable talking to you about what is going on in their lives. Ask them if they think you are helpful in their times of need or if you tend to criticize instead. And then listen to their answers without defending yourself. Now might be a good time to do that.

This will take some real courage on your part. Hearing where we have erred as parents is never easy, but it is always worth it. If they are brave enough to be truthful, thank them for their honesty even if it hurts or you think they are wrong. Just because we have been given a position of authority in their lives doesn't mean we are faultless. We need to let them know we believe that. We need to let them know that we make mistakes and that we don't think our parenting is perfect. And not in a "I know I am not perfect, *but you...*" sort of way, but rather, "I know I make mistakes, and I am willing to hear what you have to say about the way I parent." Obviously, your kids are sinners too, and their view of how you parent will be tainted by that, but are you even willing to hear what they have to say on the matter?

The gospel should make us into people who are willing to hear when we have done something wrong. The cross demonstrates that God himself had to die for our sins, so anything our kids say should pale in comparison. When you lay down your defenses and listen to your kids, they may respond in kind. This is how you create an atmosphere of grace in your home.

Mental Illness

The church, in general, has done a horrible job with mental illness. We have ignored it, pretended it doesn't exist, or worse, acted as though all mental illness was a result of sin. Our obsession with outward perfection has led us down a dark, dangerous path of contempt toward anything that doesn't measure up to our false definition of what a "good Christian" should look like.

As a parent, it can be a terrifying thought that our child is different from other kids, that our child isn't "normal." But just because they may be different doesn't mean that they are sinning. And there actually might be something different with the way their brain processes emotions—they might need more help than you or a church counselor is able to give them. If you feel shame over the fact that your kiddo needs extra help, they will sense that, and it will deepen the shame they feel for needing help. They won't understand that the shame you feel might have less to do with them and more to do with what you see as a failure in your parenting. Getting help isn't something to be ashamed of; it is just the reality of living in a broken world with broken minds.

So how do you know if your child needs extra help? If you see that your child's anxiety affects their functioning for an extended time, you need to seek medical help. For example, if your child spends more than two weeks feeling unable to go to school or attend a social function, you should seek medical attention. If your child is having reoccurring and unexpected panic attacks, you should seek medical attention. If your child is self-mutilating, you should seek medical attention. If your child is withdrawn for a long period of time, you should seek medical attention. And if your child asks for medical attention, you should seek it.

Don't just assume you know how your child is doing. Ask them. You can start with something as easy as, "I read an article that talked about the rise of anxiety in teenagers. Is this something you feel or something you are dealing with?" As parents, a lot of times we go to one of two extremes: Either we ignore a problem or we overcorrect to what might be a problem.

I typically ignore problems (because that is my personality). So if I see some things that are concerning, I just keep moving ahead, hoping everything is or will be okay. That is my sinful tendency, and it shows a real lack of trust in God. If I trusted God, I would admit and confront the problem instead of acting like it didn't exist. Acting like it doesn't exist is like saying to God, *I think this might be too much for you to do anything about.*

The other extreme I have seen parents take is to be hyperinvolved and controlling, almost to the point of not letting their child have any original thoughts or any downtime to feel. This also shows a real lack of trust in God. So much heartache could be avoided if we would just take time to listen to our children and help them identify their anxiety rather than rush to make them act appropriately. Because truth be told, our anxiety about our kids' anxiety is a lot like the beach ball metaphor I used earlier.

Stress or Anxiety?

A psychiatrist friend was kind enough to sit down and talk with me about the rise of anxiety in her patients. (Never let an author know what you do for a living!) She explained to me that a lot of kids who are identifying as anxious may just be experiencing the normal stresses of living in a broken world. Though the rise of clinical anxiety is real, there are a lot of kids who say they are anxious who do not need medical attention.

Because anxiety is in the public eye, more people are latching on to the idea that they are anxious, even when they are not. Though some of our kids might not be diagnosable as anxious, it is helpful for them to hear what other people define as anxious, as that may spark a conversation that helps you understand what they are experiencing.

The Oxford Dictionary defines stress as "a state of mental or emotional strain or tension resulting from adverse or very demanding circumstances." Stress is typically a temporary emotion that waxes or wanes depending on what is going on in your life. The temporary nature of stress is one way to differentiate it from anxiety. Stress is normally caused by outside circumstances, and when those circumstances cease to exist, the stress subsides.

For example, if I know my manuscript for a book on anxiety is due in October, I will feel stress until I finish it or at least get a good handle on its content. And yes, ironically, I am experiencing stress at the moment I'm writing this. Stress is not necessarily a bad thing; it can motivate me to write rather than watch Netflix all weekend.

While anxiety may also be caused by outside circumstances, there is a way to tell the difference:

> You can get a good reading on whether you're experiencing stress or anxiety by taking an honest assessment of what you're actually feeling. Do you feel exhausted or overwhelmed by the pressure of dealing with a school course load, work project, or a parent's expectations? That's probably stress. Do you feel a more general sense of fear or unease? Are you more worried about the future, rather than the present? Are you worried about something not too closely related to your life, or even nothing specific at all? That's more likely anxiety.[1]

If I finish my book and I still feel stress, then that is anxiety. "All anxiety disorders have one thing in common: persistent, excessive fear or worry in situations that are not threatening."[2] Being worried about being worried, being anxious about being anxious, being stressed about being stressed—these are all indicators that anxiety is the prevailing factor.

Panic attacks are other indicators of the presence of anxiety.

> Although anxiety is often accompanied by physical symptoms, such as a racing heart or knots in your stomach, what differentiates a panic attack from other anxiety symptoms is the intensity and duration of the symptoms. Panic attacks typically reach their peak level of intensity in 10 minutes or less and then begin to subside. Due to the intensity of the symptoms and their tendency to mimic those of heart disease, thyroid problems, breathing disorders, and other illnesses, people with panic disorder often make many visits to emergency rooms or doctors' offices, convinced they have a life-threatening issue.[3]

Uphill Both Ways...in the Snow

If your child is experiencing anxiety, be careful not to compare the things they may identify as stressful with the things you identify as stressful, validating yourself while dismissing them—what I call the uphill-both-ways-in-the-snow tactic. We older, more mature adults are incredibly good at this—it's when our kids complain to us about something and we respond with a drastically worse situation that we had to endure when we were younger.

> Child: "My drive to school today was hard. There was a detour, and it took forever. A bunch of us ended up

being a few minutes late to class, and the teacher was super upset with all of us. She gave every single one of us detention even though it wasn't our fault."

Parent: "You should have prepared and been on time. When I was your age, my parents couldn't afford a car, and I had to walk to school. We lived in Minnesota where it snowed 10 out of 12 months of the year. The two months it didn't snow it was over 100 degrees with 100 percent humidity. The walk to school was five miles. It was uphill both ways. If we were late, the teacher would take a wooden ruler and slap our hands with it. Then we would have to stay after and clean the outhouse because we didn't have indoor plumbing."

Okay, that story is a bit exaggerated, but you get the idea. We have conversations like this all the time. For some reason, we have a hard time validating what our kids are going through. How much effort would it take to empathize with their hardship and tell them we are sorry?

A surefire way to get your kid to stop talking to you is to make them feel stupid about their concerns. Most of us do not intend to do that—we think we are helping by putting their problem into perspective. But there is the right time to do this. While they are in the middle of opening their hearts up to you is not the right time to put them in their place. It is important for you to be available. It is important for you to be willing to just sit and listen. It is important for their home to be a safe place for them.

Socially Acceptable

If our children can't tell us about their anxiety or stress, they will find help elsewhere. Since I started writing this book, I have seen more and more celebrities, musical artists, and YouTube stars admitting to struggling with anxiety. Your kids are listening to these people too. One weekend, I was driving with my kids, and the radio announcer talked about how Shawn Mendes, a global popstar who toured with Taylor Swift, opened up about his battle with anxiety. In his single "In My Blood," he freely sings about his struggle with anxiety and the hopelessness he felt. In the song, he says he isn't going to stop fighting and he won't give up.

Logic—a rapper, songwriter, singer, and music producer—has a song called "Anziety" (be advised, there is a lot of cussing in his music) describing in detail what it is like to have an unexpected panic attack. The song starts out with a peaceful tune and a beautiful female voice singing about how life is good. Then it transitions into Logic rapping about the feelings of a panic attack. He wanted the transition to be jarring so that people understand what it is like to be doing fine and then suddenly feel anxious. With this song, he attempted to take away the taboo of mental illness, to stand next to those who deal with anxiety and say, "Me too. We will get through this."

Other popular musicians to say they have struggled with anxiety include Adele, LeAnn Rimes, Beyoncé, Taylor Swift, and John Mayer. Movie stars who have admitted to dealing with anxiety include Kristen Stewart, Oprah, Chris Evans, Emma Stone, Jennifer Lawrence, and Dakota Johnson. Some professional athletes who have admitted to feeling anxiety are Michael Phelps, Kevin Love, DeMar DeRozan, and Brandon Marshall.

Another group of celebrities that kids might turn to, and that parents need to catch up on, is YouTubers. Find out which YouTube stars your kids watch. You might be surprised at the content they are watching. Some of it is harmless and funny and helpful, some of it may not be. Ask them who they like.

Zoella, a fashion blogger on YouTube who has 12 million subscribers, has a 19-minute video where she talks about her personal experience with anxiety. It has been viewed more than four million times. Meghan Rienks, a lifestyle blogger with more than 2.3 million subscribers, has an almost 4-minute video describing what anxiety feels like. This video has close to six million views. Most of the comments for the video echo the feelings she conveyed; millions of people relate to her experience. It might be helpful to watch the video if a loved one has anxiety (though be advised, there is a swear word).

Thomas Sanders, a vlogger and internet personality who has 2.5 million subscribers, is very vocal about his struggle with anxiety. He has a video with Lilly Singh, an actress and YouTube sensation with 13 million subscribers, that deals with how to fight anxiety. The video gives some basic tips in a lighthearted way.

I hope you are getting the picture. Anxiety is a hot topic right now. If your kids are feeling anxiety and you don't help them with it, they can easily go to the internet to look for validation and support. And while these videos might be helpful to a certain extent, they leave out what truly brings hope and change for those dealing with anxiety—the healing grace of God.

Could it be that we really don't believe God has the power to help us and that is why we don't validate our kids' emotions? Is it because we are lazy and selfish and because trying to help is time-consuming and emotionally draining? Is it because we fight our own anxiety and feel helpless against its onslaught, so we don't think we can help our kids? Or is it just because life is difficult and one more problem might do us in?

Whatever the reason, I want to encourage you that you are not alone. You have a heavenly Father who sees your heart and knows your thoughts. He doesn't wonder why you aren't a better parent, caregiver, or mentor. You are his beloved. You may be tempted to shrink away from him or your children because of the guilt you feel, but resist that temptation. Draw close to him. Draw close to your kids. Remember that you are forgiven. Remember that you are loved. Remember that this isn't all there is—we are on our way home. Those thoughts will give you the courage to fight for your kids and fight to help them.

You also might be realizing that you also are experiencing anxiety.

Once again, there is no shame in getting help. Admitting weakness is a strength. Find a local counselor, talk to your pastor, ask friends for help. There is no way to help your children if you deny the fact that you need help too. If you are unsure if you or your kids need medical help, take some time now to pray. Ask the Holy Spirit to reveal to you what would be the right action to take in your circumstance. Then trust him as he guides and leads you. He is trustworthy. He is good. His love endures forever.

PART 1

How Society
Contributes to
Your Teen's Anxiety

3

Accomplishments Are King

I sat in a circle of acquaintances at an outdoor fire pit. My son, Wesley, was graduating from high school, and this was the second party I had been to that day and the fourth party in three days. I almost felt like I was in some sort of weird Groundhog Day situation—the same conversations, the same congratulations, the same forced laughter, the same veggie trays, and the same cheese and meat platters haunted every party.

Inescapably, the conversation turned to the future. I started to feel the warmth of the fire creeping up my neck and into my cheeks. I knew what was going to transpire next. Inevitably it happened: "So, Jess, what is Wesley going to do next year?" one person asked. What was the next step? What was the bigger and better thing he was moving on to?

I could almost hear him telling me how that was his least favorite question in the entire universe, how every time someone asked him about his plans, he wanted the earth to swallow him whole.

This was a boy who was the captain of his football team. Wesley taught himself to play several instruments; made all-league, first-team defense; had exceptional grades; was the recipient of parents' admiring looks...and decided that junior college was the best route for him.

I said, "He's going to live at home and attend a junior college for a couple years so he can figure out his plans."

Then I heard the follow-up question: "Oh, he isn't playing football?"

"He is coaching for the high school, but he hasn't decided whether he wants to play anymore."

That is when it got quiet. Finally, one person said, "Well, that's okay. It's good to save some money and take time to figure out what to do." Then the conversation shifted to another subject, and I sat back and thought about how much I loved my son. About how proud I was that he chose to stay home and not to go into too much debt. About how, even if he never went to college, I would still think he was one of the two most brilliant boys I had ever known.

But those thoughts never got a chance to make an appearance outside of my mind. Not that night, at least. I leaned forward and quietly listened to the other parents talk about scholarships, sports, and the amazing things their kids were up to. And I thought of my son and children in general and all the pressures they face as they grow older. I thought about the anxiety they feel to be the best or at least better than others. Then I thought about the cheese and meat platter, and I made my escape from the heat of the fire pit.

The Rise of Youth Sports

"Three out of four American families with school-aged children have at least one playing an organized sport—a total of about 45 million kids."[1] Perhaps this is true for your family too. Almost everyone is playing organized sports. In my own family, all three of my children are involved in organized sports. My oldest is currently playing football for a local junior college (yes, he decided to play after all), my middle son plays football for his high school, and my daughter plays softball in a community rec league. I have nothing against kids playing sports, and I think it is beneficial on a lot of different levels: It can aid character building and can be physically advantageous. But our national obsession with our kids playing sports is out of hand. Actually, let me rephrase that— our national obsession with kids *excelling* at sports is out of hand.

Just today, my brother was telling me about a news article he read about a 14-year-old eighth-grade boy who was 6 feet 7 inches and 370 pounds. This boy had verbal commitments from five colleges. He was being extolled for his quickness and strength. His size and ability might have made him a hot commodity, but I doubt that many people were considering his humanness, his middle-school brain.

He isn't the only one who feels the effects of this. Kids as young as 13 are being pursued by colleges across the nation. LeBron James publicly stated that he wanted colleges to stop pursuing his 10-year-old son. Those are extreme examples, but if you have been at any youth sports games, you've heard the parents talk about their children with such a reverence, you would think they are talking about an MLB superstar.

In every high school, a few kids stand out because they are great athletes. Kids wear their all-star gear everywhere they go. One of the first questions kids get asked is "Do you play sports? Which ones?" The assumption is that most kids play several sports, and the older they get, the more they are inclined to put all their effort into excelling at just one. Is it because we are becoming a nation obsessed with getting into a good college? Is it because the fame and fortune of being a professional athlete are so alluring? Or is it just because the magnetism of being better than someone—anyone—is all we can think about?

I know of several different high schools that bend the rules for their athletes. They don't abide by state regulations that make sure that student athletes are getting the grades they should. The coaches think winning is more important than kids passing their English class. They may not flat-out break the rules, but they "strongly encourage" other boys on the football team to "help" their teammate with his homework. Though the coaches may not explicitly state it, the message is loud and clear: The star athlete must not be sidelined due to grades. There is even a trend to lower the 2.0 grade point average requirement so more kids can play.

The constant praise of athletic accomplishments is communicating to our kids that their worth is tied up in how they perform on the field.

The worship of professional athletes is communicating that fame and fortune are the pinnacles of human success. Of course, this creates anxiety. When a child fails, strikes out, fumbles the ball, misses the putt, or whatever, they feel the disappointment of everyone around them. Conversely, when they succeed, they have an inflated sense of accomplishment. Neither of those is a good thing. Part of the benefit of sports is to learn to be a team player and keep an even temperament whether you win or lose. This is a good life skill. But too much emphasis on performance will end in too much stress or anxiety for a kid.

Academics

As if athletic pressure wasn't enough, children also have the pressure to perform well academically. The college admissions process is out of control. And as early as third grade, kids are challenged to know what college they want to attend. Some private and charter schools require children to pass tests and have personal interviews before they are even considered for admission. Some well-intentioned teachers ask their students to bring in pennants of their preferred college, which are then placed all around the classroom as reminders that their future is looming.

The teachers themselves are often pressured to get the kids to score high on standardized tests. If their classroom fails, then the school fails, and the teachers feel as though they have failed. Standardized testing is on the rise. In 2002, the No Child Left Behind Act required states to test and rate schools to determine how much federal funding they get. In 2009, the pressure escalated with the Race to the Top grant. The program split a pool of $4.35 billion between the winning schools. In order to receive this funding, states had to rate teachers as good or bad based on their students' standardized test scores.

I always know when the school is giving these tests because not only do they send an email communicating how important it is that my kid gets enough rest and eats right during the testing but also because my kids are visibly more stressed during that time. An email I received talked about the "testing season" that would take place from April 24 to May 21. The email closed out with this sentence: "We are quite proud of the learning that has been going on all year long, and this is an opportunity for our Rams to shine." If that is what they are sending out to the parents, you know the kids are hearing it every day.

My daughter has an individualized education plan (IEP) to help with her memory-related learning disability, so she is considerably more anxious during these testing times. She talks about how she feels the need to achieve good scores for the school. These tests have absolutely nothing to do with children's grades, and yet so much emphasis is placed on them. I asked her how she felt during these tests. At first, she just said, "Stupid," but when I pressed to tell me more, she elaborated:

> I feel helpless. Like everything I've worked for just crumbles away with a question I can't read or an equation I can't remember how to solve. I feel like I'll never get smarter or more educated. I mean, I've always been bad, mainly because I can't remember anything. When I sit there and look at the computer, I don't really see a test. I just see a bunch of mistakes waiting to happen. I know when I get a problem wrong, and the fact that I have to keep going and keep failing just makes me feel worse. Having one standardized test that labels you as smart or dumb, advanced or behind—it's devastating because it lays it all right in front of you. Not everyone learns or works in the same way, so if you can't give thousands of people the same medication to help all their individual problems, you can't test thousands of different strengths and weaknesses on the same test. It might help with data, but it makes kids feel stupid. Because clearly you aren't smart because you failed the big final, right?[2]

Again, she is only in eighth grade, and this is the weight she feels during these tests. She has enough trouble with her own classes without feeling the pressure from these other tests.

> A typical student takes 112 mandated standardized tests between pre-kindergarten classes and 12th grade, a new Council of the Great City Schools study found. By contrast, most countries that outperform the United States on international exams test students three times during their school careers.[3]

The disparity in the number of tests taken is vast. I don't have enough knowledge to say if the tests ultimately help or hurt, but I do know that they add more stress for our children. I also want to make it very clear that I am grateful for the public school system. I have homeschooled my kids and sent them to a private school, and I know that every schooling option has its pitfalls. So please don't read this as a condemnation of public schools. We would be lost without the help they have given my daughter—help that I couldn't provide myself. My purpose here is solely to highlight some of the sources that may cause our children anxiety.

The pressure for our children to get into their desired college is all-consuming, and the admission process is ludicrous. Kids who have 4.0 GPAs, started on varsity in their local high schools, and completed tons of volunteer hours are being denied admittance in the schools of their choice. College acceptance rates have dropped dramatically for several reasons. The internet makes the application process easier, so more kids are applying. Kids from other nations are applying to schools in the United States, so now the competition is global. Colleges keep their acceptance rates low to add a sense of prestige. In the excellent book *Where You Go Is Not Who You'll Be*, author Frank Bruni writes,

> Somewhere along the way, a school's selectiveness— measured in large part by its acceptance rate—became

synonymous with its worth. Acceptance rates are prominently featured in the profiles of schools that appear in various reference books and surveys, including the raptly monitored one by *U.S. News & World Report*, whose annual ranking of American colleges factor in those rates slightly. Colleges know that many prospective applicants equate a lower acceptance rate with a more coveted, special and brag-worthy experience, and these colleges endeavor to bring their rates down by ratcheting up the number of young people who apply. They bang the drums like never before. From the organization that administers the SAT, they buy the names of students who have scored above a certain mark and are at least remotely plausible, persuadable applicants, then they send those students pamphlets and literature that grow glossier and more alluring—*that leafy quadrangle! those gleaming microscopes!*—by the year. The college admissions office is no longer a screening committee. It's a ruthlessly efficient purveyor of Ivory Tower porn.[4]

The cost of college tuition is on the rise as well. "The nation's top 50 private universities, as ranked by *U.S. News and World Report*, are upping their tuition by an average of 3.6%. A handful are even raising their tuition rates by more than 4%, according to their websites."[5] The rate of increased tuition is often higher than the rate of inflation. So kids worry about not only whether they can get into a good college but also whether they can afford it. They must decide if it is worth it to take on student loans to get a good education, which would (hopefully) lead to better jobs to provide for their families.

There are student loans available to help with education, but only about 2 percent of high school students are awarded athletic scholarships,[6] and only about 19 percent of kids with a GPA of 3.5 to 4.0 get awarded academic scholarships.[7] The competition is fierce.

When I asked my college-age son how he feels about transferring to a university when he completes junior college, he replied,

> It's not that I necessarily feel the pressure to get into a great college. It's pressure to just get into a college, period. Because it's so hard and so expensive. Getting a degree is expensive no matter how you slice it. That's why I am doing junior college for two years. I'm trying to pay the least to make the most. But that's very stressful. I want to be able to support a family.

Society emphasizes going to a great school so you can get a great job, have lots of money, and live a great life. But there are many people who don't go to college at all and are very successful, many who go to trade schools and end up doing what they love for the rest of their lives, and many who live modest lives but are happy, which should equal success. But in our society, we seem to think that success is defined by more time in college, more academic accolades, and more awards.

Social Activism

Another prominent factor contributing to teen anxiety is the societal call to be involved in a greater cause. Again, this isn't necessarily a bad thing, but kids are being asked to fill their free time (as if they had a ton of free time, considering their sports and academic obligations) with volunteering.

Time magazine puts out a list every year of the 30 most influential teens. I read through the past few lists, and even I felt incredibly inadequate—all my accomplishments in my 40-plus years of life seemed like nothing compared to some of these kids, who have multimillion-dollar companies or have raised awareness for noble causes.

The bigger the platform, the bigger the influence, the better off you are—that is the message from society. You need a message, and you need to shout it from the mountaintops or your Twitter account. It's not just about making money; it's about being passionate about something that needs fixing. It's about the rise of social activism.

The kids who survived the horrific Marjory Stoneman Douglas High School shooting have organized gun control rallies just from social media apps. Cameron Kasky now has 387,300 followers on Twitter, Kai Koerber has 18,000, Alex Wind has 54,100, Chris Grady has 22,700, and Sofie Whitney has 46,300. These are just a few of the teens who have used the tragedy to advance the fight for gun control. Imagine the pressure they must feel to stay relevant.

This is not a commentary on their views or my own. Instead, I'm fascinated by the way social media has changed our culture and the pressure it can put on kids. The students in Columbine didn't have the platform to immediately express their concerns to the world. For kids in Parkland, silence online was hardly an option. Please don't get me wrong—speaking out against social issues can be a good thing, but the pressure to do it is contributing to anxiety.

Hope and Peace

With these three societal pressures—sports, academics, and social activism—closing in on our kids, we need to be able to offer them a place of peace. They need to hear from their caregivers, parents, and mentors that their identities do not rest on how well they hit, catch, or kick a ball, or tackle, or anything they do on the field of competition. They need to hear that the college they attend doesn't make them a more valuable person. They need to hear that even if they decide to never attend college, they are still loved. They need to hear that they don't have to use every circumstance to further a cause. They need to hear that they don't have to be one of *Time*'s top 30 influential teens in order to matter. They need to hear that they matter because they were created in the image of God. They matter because they are loved and valued.

If your kids are involved in sports, make sure they know you love them regardless of their performance. Ask them if they feel pressure from you or anxiety when they play. Ask them if they feel pressure from the coaches or the other players. Give them an open door to discuss how they are feeling on the field, court, or rink. Don't downplay their feelings; just listen. Do what you can to validate what they are saying and then point them to their only hope. Tell them that what they do on that field will not determine whether they will have a successful, God-glorifying life. Define success outside of performance.

Before your kids go off to school or as they sit down at the dining room table to be homeschooled, tell them their grades are not indicators of their worth. Make sure they hear you say that no matter how many questions they get wrong on a test, they are still loved. Make sure the message they get from you is not that higher education somehow equals a more valuable life. It doesn't. Make sure you know that for yourself as well. Tell them that their identities are not wrapped up in a test score. If they have learning disabilities, explain to them that God knows and sees how difficult education is for them, and he is with them, helping, leading, and guiding them.

If your child has a heart for social activism, encourage them, but also reassure them that they can't win every battle and that the success of their campaign, whatever it may be, will not determine how much God or you love them. Let them know that even while they attempt to do big things, the biggest thing has already been done for them—Christ's sacrifice on the cross.

Wonderfully Made

Psalm 139:13-18 offers life-giving, hope-building words for those who think their performance determines their value:

> For you formed my inward parts;
>   you knitted me together in my mother's womb.

I praise you, for I am fearfully and wonderfully made.
Wonderful are your works;
   my soul knows it very well.
My frame was not hidden from you,
when I was being made in secret,
   intricately woven in the depths of the earth.
Your eyes saw my unformed substance;
in your book were written, every one of them,
   the days that were formed for me,
   when as yet there was none of them.
How precious to me are your thoughts, O God!
   How vast is the sum of them!
If I would count them, they are more than the sand.
   I awake, and I am still with you.

In The Message, Eugene Peterson offers the following translation:

Oh yes, you shaped me first inside, then out;
   you formed me in my mother's womb.
I thank you, High God—you're breathtaking!
   Body and soul, I am marvelously made!
   I worship in adoration—what a creation!
You know me inside and out,
   you know every bone in my body;
You know exactly how I was made, bit by bit,
   how I was sculpted from nothing into something.
Like an open book, you watched me grow from conception
     to birth;
   all the stages of my life were spread out before you,
The days of my life all prepared
   before I'd even lived one day.
Your thoughts—how rare, how beautiful!
   God, I'll never comprehend them!

> I couldn't even begin to count them—
>   any more than I could count the sand of the sea.
> Oh, let me rise in the morning and live always with you!

Let your kids hear you say that the way they are made, flaws and all, is fearful (awesome) and wonderful because their Maker is fearful (awesome) and wonderful. Tell them they aren't an accident and that every single part of them—physically, emotionally, and spiritually—was made with purpose by God. Tell them that every single day of their life was written in his book even before they were born and that their accomplishments and failures are all given to them by the design of God.

Tell them he thinks about them. How crazy is that? The God of the universe thinks about them all the time. The number of his thoughts about them is vast. Tell them that if they are living, they are with him. His promise to never leave or forsake them follows them on the field, into the classroom, and throughout their life.

If they wonder what God thinks of them, tell them to look at Jesus; God's thoughts toward us all are embodied in the life, death, and resurrection of Christ. What does he give to show you his love? Everything. His love does not fluctuate depending on performance. His thoughts are forever ones of love. He has made a covenant with his people and will not forsake it.

You see, there is only one place where our kids don't have to perform, and that is before the Holy God, who sent his Son to perform on our behalf so that we and our kids stand perfect in his sight. Give your kids a place of rest. Give them a place they don't have to perform. Give them Jesus.

4

The Disdain of Being Normal

A quick search online provides a long list of inspiring quotes about reaching for the stars. For example...

> *"Only I can change my life. No one can do it for me."*
> —Carol Burnett

> *"Good, better, best, never let it rest 'til your good is better, and your better best."*
> —often attributed to Saint Jerome

> *"Failure will never overtake me if my determination to succeed is strong enough."*
> —Og Mandino

> *"If you can dream it, you can do it."*
> —Walt Disney

> *"It always seems impossible until it's done."*
> —Nelson Mandela

> *"Set your goals high; don't stop until you get there."*
> —Bo Jackson

"I want to be the best."

—Odell Beckham Jr.

"The will to win, the desire to succeed, the urge to reach your full potential...these are the keys that will unlock the door to personal excellence."

—Confucius

Some popular hashtags communicate the same idea:

#bestdayever
#bestmomever
#bestmealever
#bestdadever
#beststudentever
#bestbestever
#bestvacationever
#besthusbandever
#bestwifeever
#bestdateever

We are repeatedly hammered with encouragements to be the best—the best everything ever. We see it on social media posts. We hear it when people describe someone or something. We see it in photos they post. The desire to be the best, own the best things, or have the best time is in all of us, and it has the tendency to become a motivating factor in what we do. Advertisement agencies know that this is exactly how to grab your attention:

"Want to be the best runner you can be? Buy our running shoes!"

"Want to be the best writer you can be? Buy our online course about writing."

"Want to be the best mom? Read our book!"

"Want to be the best student? Let us tutor you!"

"Want to reach your full potential? We will coach you on how to become all that you can be!"

The call to be perfect is pushing kids into anxiety.

> [Perfectionism] is a steady source of negative emotions; rather than reaching toward something positive, those in its grip are focused on the very thing they most want to avoid—negative evaluation. Perfectionism, then, is an endless report card; it keeps people completely self-absorbed, engaged in perpetual self-evaluation—reaping relentless frustration and doomed to anxiety and depression.[1]

You may be wondering how "be your best" relates to perfectionism. Perfectionism is the logical endgame if all our kids ever hear is "be your best you." It's no coincidence that this mentality and anxiety are both on the rise.

You know the scenario. You open your favorite social media app, and you see a post of your friend (the one who just ran her tenth marathon, posted pics all along the way, got her best time, and never broke a sweat) standing with her 16-year-old kid—a model—in front of the most beautiful seascape in Ireland.

Her son won a trip to Ireland because of an essay he wrote on being the change you want to see in the world. Ironically, they are your only friends who could actually afford a trip to Ireland, but that is beside the point. He is wearing his letterman's jacket with so many patches proclaiming his excellencies, you can't even make out his school colors. The caption reads,

> So proud of Brock! He won us this beautiful trip to Ireland. He is so dedicated though that between his workouts, all the schoolwork, and his obsession with filling out college applications, we have barely had time to do very much sightseeing. LOL! Oh well. Hopefully he will

make enough money one day to take us all back here to make up for it. JK JK. Today we did get to tour a lovely seaside castle. We are so proud of the man who our son is becoming, we decided to gift him with a cottage here. He immediately told us that with the cottage, he wanted to start a home for underprivileged youth. So today we are researching how to make that happen. #allglorytoGod #bethechange

Though this example is exaggerated, you know you have seen posts that were similar. You see this type of character in almost every modern movie: the classic overachiever who is never satisfied with being the best. I am about to date myself, but Jessie Spano from *Saved by the Bell* is a great example of this. Topanga from *Boy Meets World*, Spencer from *Pretty Little Liars*, and Betty from *Riverdale* all fit this mold. These characters are all obsessed with being better than. They all must get into the best colleges. They all must look perfect all the time. They all must be viewed as the one with all the right answers. If they don't get any of these things, they have huge mental breakdowns.

A recent study from the American Psychological Association, "Perfectionism Is Increasing over Time," states that teens are experiencing more anxiety from perfectionism now than ever before. Psychologists Andrew Hill and Thomas Curran consider perfectionism "a cultural phenomenon." The authors found that kids today believe the perfect life is attainable if you have the right achievements, social status, and wealth—you just have to try hard enough to get it. Kids feel they have to attain others' approval to achieve this level of success. The study states that "perfectionism is conceived as a misguided attempt to procure others' approval and repair feelings of unworthiness and shame through displays of high achievement."[2]

In other words, our kids believe that if they can just get people to see how successful they are, they will feel worthy of adoration. In direct contrast, they constantly feel unworthiness and shame because they don't think they are measuring up. They define themselves by how extraordinary they can become. They set incredibly high standards and unattainable goals, and then they crash and burn when they can't reach them.

Hill and Curran came up with a few reasons they believe that kids are falling into the trap of perfectionism. They believe, and I concur, that "young people also appear now to be more self-interested and spend less time doing group activities for fun and more time doing individual activities for instrumental value or sense of personal achievement": taking private lessons, spending time on their phones, playing video games, being tutored, studying, and so on. It looks as though teens have become obsessed "with upward social comparison, experience considerable status anxiety, and adopt materialism as a means of perfecting their lives in relation to others." This is teenagers' new rat race: look the best—or at least better than your friends—befriend the most popular people, and get into the best college, and just like that, you win. That's the point—to win. Individualism is a key component when it comes to perfectionism.

With the constant drive to be the best, just being good at something is no longer desirable. Society disdains being average. It's either be the best or don't do it at all. Why be mediocre? If doing something to the best of your abilities isn't perfect, is it worth doing? Society has begun to realize how ridiculous it is to expect perfection in huge things, so now it is turning its eye toward being the best in simple things.

Real Simple is one of the most popular magazines around. Its pages are full of easy ways to do extraordinary things while keeping everything very simple and neat. The *New York Times* bestseller *The Life-Changing Magic of Tidying Up: The Japanese Art of Decluttering and Organizing* boasts that if you learn properly how to "simplify and organize your home once, you'll never have to do it again." This stripping down isn't really a stripping down at all; you are still striving for being perfect at simplicity.

In his insightful book *Bobos in Paradise: The New Upper Class and How They Got There*, David Brooks says this about American individualism:

What is most absolute is not truth and falsehood, virtue and vice; what matters most absolutely is the advancing of self. The individual is perpetually moving toward wholeness and completion, and ideas are adopted as they suit that mission. Individual betterment is the center around which the entire universe revolves.

This is a brutal form of narcissism. The weight of the universe is placed on the shoulders of the individual. Accordingly, in modern American culture, the self becomes semidivinized.[3]

We can't be our own gods. We can't bear the pressure of trying to be our own saviors.

The burden to seem flawless has been growing since the early 2000s. Researchers have examined how two types of perfectionism have spiked in the last few years. The first is self-oriented: "I must be my best self all the time or I am a failure and not worth anything." The second is oriented toward others: "You need to get your act together and be better, and if you don't, I am going to treat you like the piece of trash you are." You can see how either of those lines of thinking will ruin the lives of young adults, hurting the way they think of themselves and the way they think of others. This makes relationships very difficult and feeds an overblown individualism.

Most perfectionists are constantly looking for the approval of those around them. They need consistent affirmation. When they think they have failed others, they feel a sense of disapproval. Again, this is harmful to relationships and to their own mental health. It leads to anxiety and feeling like there is always something more to be done to win the favor and approval of others.

Perfectionism pits failure and success against each other, when in reality, they go hand in hand. Everything is an extreme: "I must always excel" and "I must never fail." If they aren't at the front of the pack, they feel like failures. This extreme competitiveness proves that nobody really wins. It is debilitating and pushes them further into anxiety or depression.

What they miss is that learning from failure builds a person's character and fortitude. When we fail, we must figure out what was wrong with the way we did things previously and adapt. We also must learn to push through the negative emotions that come with failing. This teaches us that our performance is just one facet of who we are.

But the perfectionist avoids failure at all costs, thus depriving themselves of the very thing they need—the truth that "success hinges less on getting everything right than on how you handle getting things wrong. This is where creativity, passion, and perseverance come into play."[4]

Perfectionism turns people into achievement slaves. And don't think for a minute that means that they are always go-getters. Sometimes perfectionists just stop trying all together. *If I can't do it perfectly, I just won't do it at all.* We think of perfectionists as high achieving, but for many, their fear of failure paralyzes them. Jenni Berrett is one such person. She describes the process like this:

> You start a project determined to execute it perfectly. You avoid it until you can "do it right," but then you don't do it at all. You feel frozen, stuck, incapable. You are *paralyzed* by the fear that you will be bad at the thing you want to accomplish. Which, of course, makes it impossible to accomplish anything.
>
> It's a never-ending cycle: perfectionism, procrastination, paralysis...
>
> I recede further and further inside myself.[5]

We shouldn't always assume that because our kids don't get their work done, they are lazy. It could be that the fear of failure prevents them from completing the job.

The other side of this perfectionism coin is obsessive-compulsive disorder (OCD). I am sure you have heard stories of OCD or perhaps even have children who suffer from it. OCD ultimately stems from the desire for everything to be exactly as it should be, the desire for perfection. Sara Kelley describes what it was like for her as an 11-year-old struggling with OCD:

> I would wake up at 5:50 on the nose. Not a minute before, not a minute after. I'd dash into the kitchen and begin making a pot of coffee for my mother. I would prepare everything the night before—the filter already filled with fresh coffee grounds, the water container already filled to the line, the spoon perfectly aligned on a fresh napkin. While waiting for the coffee to brew, I would prepare and eat my breakfast. When the coffee was finished, I'd pour it into a cup and place it to the right of my mother's "spot" at the kitchen table, with the handle perfectly aligned to the right. By 6:05, I HAD to be finished in the kitchen and on my way to my next morning task. I'd get dressed, brush my teeth, make my bed, curl the tips of my hair, and run to the living room to start my next morning ritual. At exactly 6:30, I would turn on the television and watch QVC (the home shopping network). The show was so structured, which was appealing to me. I was fascinated as to how they could talk about one single item for an hour straight, without it seeming too repetitive or mundane. The show brought me an odd sense of comfort, which is why I let it into my life every single day. At 7:20, I would grab my backpack, head to the car, and mentally prepare myself for a day of school.[6]

This self-imposed pressure was unbearable for her. She goes on to write about how OCD dominated her life. If you don't know someone with OCD, a quick search online will yield plenty of articles describing what it feels like for them. We often live with the mantra that "every day matters"; well, for those suffering from OCD, every *second* matters.

Our Ordinary Lives and His Surpassing Power

How do we help our kids combat this temptation to want to exceed all expectations? How do we tell them that ordinary is okay? The apostle Paul addresses this very thing in 2 Corinthians 4:7: "But we have this treasure in jars of clay, to show that the surpassing power belongs to God and not to us." Eugene Peterson offers this paraphrase:

> If you only look at *us*, you might well miss the brightness. We carry this precious Message around in the unadorned clay pots of our ordinary lives. That's to prevent anyone from confusing God's incomparable power with us. As it is, there's not much chance of that. You know for yourselves that we're not much to look at (MSG).

We are all free to be "unadorned clay pots." We are free to have "ordinary lives." Why is that? Because it is about God's surpassing power. The power of the gospel. The power of the good news of what Jesus has done for us.

There is no reason to despise the ordinary. Tell your kids that their everyday routine is not something to be sneered at. Turning off the alarm in the morning and dragging your body out of bed go to school, doing homework, going to practices—these ordinary events are not to be undervalued or overlooked. You don't have to be the flashiest; you are free to be an unadorned clay pot.

Why? Because you aren't the prize here. Being the best student, pianist, soccer player, son, daughter, sister, or brother is not the point. The point is that we have a God who delights in using ordinary means to show off his surpassing power so we know that the power belongs to

God and not to amazing methods or strategies for living. Nothing is wrong with those things, but if anyone puts their hope in them, they will be disappointed. If you place your identity in a label—student, athlete, musician, actor, nerd, emo, whatever—not only will you walk away with a broken heart, but you will hurt those around you. Your job is to be an ordinary pot. In the book *Liturgy of the Ordinary*, Tish Harrison Warren says this:

> Christ's ordinary years are a part of our redemption story. Because of the incarnation and those long, unrecorded years of Jesus' life, our small, normal lives matter. If Christ was a carpenter, all of us who are in Christ find that our work is sanctified and made holy. If Christ spent time in obscurity, then there is infinite worth found in obscurity...There is no task too small or too routine to reflect God's glory and worth.[7]

Teach your kids that their vocation or calling is holy. It doesn't matter what the calling is—be it a student, an athlete, a barista, or a grocery bagger. We need to teach our kids that their work is sacred and that it matters. They are serving the community and making it a better place just by going to school. God uses people in seemingly ordinary ways to make the community flourish.

A lot of Christ's life was spent in the everyday, ordinary practices of being a carpenter. This ordinary life is opposite to how we think things should go. There is rest there. There is courage there. Tell your kids that going to school matters, but not because of the college they might get into or the test they need to get a good grade on; going to school matters because it is what God has called them to do. Their learning is important not just for them but for the whole of society. However, God has gifted them to learn—whether it comes easy or it is incredibly difficult—they go to school because it is their vocation, and their vocation or calling is straight from God to them. He has made them for this moment and this school, and faithfully fulfilling that vocation is a beautiful thing.

An Everlasting Perfection

How do you free someone who is constantly striving for perfection? You tell them that they already have it. In Christ, we are seen as completely perfect. In Matthew 3, we read the story of Jesus being baptized. Two key phrases in this passage stand out and will give the perfectionist hope.

First, John asks Jesus why he is the one who gets to baptize Jesus. John feels he should be baptized *by* Jesus, not the other way around; he sees his own imperfection. But Jesus responds with this in verse 15: "Let it be so now, for thus it is fitting for us to fulfill all righteousness." Jesus fulfills our righteousness. He was baptized on our behalf. He did it so that he could live the perfect life that we were meant to live. He did this so that we could stand before the Holy God as one who is righteous.

Second, in verse 17, when Jesus comes out of the water, a voice from heaven says, "This is my beloved Son, with whom I am well pleased." Why is that significant? Because the Bible tells us that we are in Christ. So what God the Father thinks of God the Son, God the Father also thinks of us. Anyone who believes is God's beloved child in whom he is well pleased. Jesus's work earned that. He lived the perfect life that the Bible demands us to live. He died for every single one of our imperfections so that now all those who are hidden in Christ are seen as completely perfect. That is glorious news. That is news we should tell our kids.

So instead of giving into the message "Work, work, work and always be the best, best, best," let's relax into the message of the Bible, which is that our performance isn't what makes us perfect. Christ's death on the cross earns us the status of "perfect" before the only one who really matters.

5

Social Media, Electronics, and Our Kids

I am currently sitting in a local coffee shop, and I am completely distracted by a group of 15- or 16-year-old girls sitting at the table next to me. I am sure you can guess what they are doing. They are on their eighth selfie. *Eighth!* You know the scene—you've seen it before. You may have even participated in it. They take dozens of poses, they move around to find better lighting, they hold their coffee cups up for a Boomerang video, and so on.

"O-M-G. You look so hot in that one, but my chin looks so weird."

"It doesn't! But look at my weird hand placement!"

"I think we are all super gorg."

The scrutiny that each picture gets after it is taken is more intense than the love that Sméagol feels for the ring. They finally get a picture everyone can agree on. It's picture number ten. And now they group-message the pic so everyone can start editing it to make sure they look like the prettiest one in the group.

I don't know if they really did that; I just know that even my group of friends do that...and we can't blame the vanity on being young. I also know that I am always slightly annoyed with the one person who always wants to take the picture over and over until they take the right one—well, until I see the pic they chose, that is. Then I am pleased. It's a good pic. We all look good (or as good as we can). We all look happy. I guess all the retakes were really worth it. And just like that, it's time to post.

I can roll my eyes at those teenagers (such an old lady thing to write), but the truth is I am just like them. We are all, every one of us, looking to put our best selves, or selfies, forward. Every single one of us tries to create an image or a scene that will generate a specific feeling in those who see it, whether that is jealousy, pride, desire, or whatever it is—we all want to be well thought of. And that is another contributing factor to the rise in anxiety in the last ten years.

It's Not All Bad

Before I continue, I need to say that I love my iPhone. I will not try to convince you and your kids to revert to using a flip phone. One of my goals with this book is to stay away from scare tactics. There is a big enough problem without me adding to the hyperbole that the world is falling apart because of smartphones. I do not want to induce anxiety in a book about how to help fight anxiety. So as I address the dangers of electronics and smartphones, I want to be very clear that I firmly believe they can be very helpful. Even to and maybe especially for kids with anxiety.

Social media can be a place to find others who have the same interests or maybe even the same problems, and in these like-minded communities, people learn from each other. Of course, this can be good or bad depending on the community. I know of several people who have posted about their own mental illnesses or particular struggles, and I have watched as others have spoken up and shared their own experiences or offered words of encouragement to the posters.

Social media has leveled the playing field so that people who at one time didn't have a voice now do. Issues that once were kept quiet or hidden are now being talked about openly. People who need help with various expenses—be they medical expenses, funeral costs, or car payments—put up GoFundMe pages, and they receive support from people around the internet. And never underestimate the power of a hilarious meme to change the direction of a bad day.

Social media isn't an evil force, but it is something we should be wise about. So please, let me caution you from being extreme with your kid's electronics after you read this chapter. I have a dear friend who is always encouraging me to walk the wobbly middle. Don't go to one extreme—*Never use social media!*—or the other—*Social media is always the best!* Rather, prayerfully and prudently figure out what is best for your family. Sometimes you will veer toward one extreme, and other times you will veer toward the other, but try your best to stay in the middle, living a life in single devotion to Christ.

Smartphone Society

The first iPhone was released in 2007. Around the time, teens started reporting feeling more anxious the more time they spend on electronics.

> On any given day, American teenagers (13- to 18-year-olds) average about nine hours (8:56) of entertainment media use, excluding time spent at school or for homework. Tweens (8- to 12-year-olds) use an average of about six hours' (5:55) worth of entertainment media daily.[1]

When I read that, I gasped. My immediate response was "Surely not." Then I sat back and thought, "Well, yes. I guess that does make sense." From watching a show, to scrolling through social media, to listening to music, to looking for a new outfit, to watching videos on Instagram or Facebook, to playing video games, I can see how a kid might spend over half their day using media.

Spending time in front of a screen is not new to teens. Since the invention of the television, kids have spent loads of time consuming media. The difference is now we can get all that media anywhere, as long as we have our mobile devices, and now we can consume it alone. When I was a kid, my family would have to find a show that everyone wanted to watch together. If you didn't like the show that the majority picked, you just had two options: you could sit through the show, or you could find something else to do.

Now you can watch whatever you want all the time. You can listen to whatever music you like all the time. This allows individualism to run wild, which in turn encourage loneliness, which in turn encourages anxiety. Our kids are retreating further into themselves. Whenever anyone does this, they open themselves up to only one voice—their own. Typically, our internal voices aren't very encouraging. Just today, my own anxious thoughts have included the following:

"You don't have enough time today to do everything you need."

"You aren't going to do that right—you always screw that up."

"Look at how fit that girl is! You should exercise more."

On and on my inner lawyer works on condemning me. It wasn't until a dear friend asked me if I was doing okay that I even realized I was letting my anxious thoughts take over my heart. We need voices outside of ourselves speaking into our lives, and our teens do as well. While we often think that alone time will help us—and don't get me wrong, alone time can be very profitable—too much alone time can shut out the help around us and make us feel like we don't have any-body...even though being alone was our choice.

As a parent, I will confess that even though I see the dangers in this, I also really love the peace and quiet of everyone happily doing their own thing with their own earbuds in. It is a real temptation for me to assume that since no one is complaining or showing unhappiness, all my kids are doing great mentally. We must do the hard work of talking to our kids and engaging them about their media use. It is as simple as asking them to play you their favorite song or watch an episode of their favorite show with you. Or if you really want to be confounded by society, ask them to show you a video from their favorite YouTuber, or maybe even try your hand at playing their latest video game obsession.

Doing any one of these things will give you a real look into what they are doing with most of their time. Plus, it would give you something to talk about, and who knows, you might even enjoy what they enjoy, which would create some common ground for a relationship. It would also ease the isolation-induced anxiety I spoke about earlier. Having something in common with your kids will bring them out of that. Even if it is as minuscule as liking the same song they like—that strengthens your connection with them. We are made for community, and we thrive in it. Solitary confinement is used as a punishment for prisoners because being alone isn't how we are created to be.

Social Media

When I first started talking with my kids about writing this book, I asked them what they thought caused the most anxiety in teens. Without hesitation, my daughter piped up with, "Social media. For sure. Especially Instagram." And while most of our teens are on social media, only 10 percent of them say it is their favorite way to spend their time. Still, they partake in it every single day.

If so few of them really enjoy it, why are they still on it? The answer is FOMO. If you aren't familiar with that term, it means "fear of missing out." They must know what is going on in everyone's life so they can talk about it at school and feel included—they can't miss out on anything.

The truth of the matter is that the perfectly curated feeds of their friends don't really represent what is going on in their lives. That group of girls I mentioned at the beginning of the chapter were attempting to show what a great time they were having drinking coffee and talking. The truth of the matter was they hadn't taken a sip of their coffee and hadn't talked to each other at all except to give directions on a new pose for a pic. I can almost guarantee that the coffee was cold by the time they got to it.

Often when I post something on social media, my friends will comment on it the next time I see them. They often say, "The party/event/concert you went to looked like it was so much fun." My comment back is always the same: "That's the point of social media." Then we both laugh, and I tell them how horrible the event/party/concert really was and that I just snapped a picture when we were at the zenith of our enjoyment.

Now, they know I am mostly joking, but I also do want to call to light the fact that the pictures are meant to look fun or beautiful or whatever. Parul Sehgal, a book critic for the *New York Times*, said this in a Ted Talk in 2013: "We live in jealous times. We are all good citizens of social media, where the currency in envy."[2]

Anxiety didn't start because of Instagram. Anxious teens have been around since the very beginning of time. But it certainly does exacerbate the problem. Instagram gives them a way to feed the anxiousness in their hearts, a way that wasn't there before smartphones. Social media is exposing the deeply rooted problem of looking to others for fulfillment and acceptance and the tendency to compare and despair. Constantly seeing the best part of your friends' lives—however staged—makes trying to be okay with your own life very difficult.

Our kids are living in jealous times. They can see the parties they weren't invited to. They see the perfect picture from the perfect angle with the perfect filter, and then they look in the mirror and are confronted with their flaws. When we were younger, if our friends got together outside of school and we weren't invited, we didn't know about it. Our kids can't escape that knowledge. This feeling of not measuring up or not fitting in contributes to anxiety and depression.

We need to have a strong understanding of how social media affects the ways our kids feel. It may be a good time to put the book down and have a conversation with your kid about this. Understand that they might be resistant to talking to you honestly about it because they may think you will take it away from them. Assure them you just want to know them better. Ask them how social media makes them feel. Ask them if they ever struggle with their emotions or feel left out when they use social media. This is probably more of a concern for girls, but that doesn't mean boys don't feel it too.

Uncomfortable Emotions

When I was I kid, I learned early on that the two words I never wanted to say to my parents were "I'm bored"—to say this would lead to a list of chores to help ease my boredom. Many people have had this experience. I have also heard many parents respond to this complaint by saying "Only boring people are bored."

Kids today never have to deal with being bored because they are constantly entertained. Because they don't have to work through boredom or some other uncomfortable feelings, they become less skilled at dealing with their emotions. Before social media, when we were feeling bored or lonely, we found ways to connect with people. This forced us to confront our anxiety about making friends.

When I was about 12, we moved to a new city. I didn't know anyone in the area, so whenever I felt bored, I could either stay inside and risk being given chores or go outside and try to befriend the kids on the street. I had to decide that the possibility of being rejected by the kids outside was better than sitting inside. I had to take the risk. I had to learn how to be friendly with people I didn't know.

Kids today don't face that problem. They can just go to their online communities, where they know they will find acceptance, or text their friends from school or church. When they text, they pick out the right words before they reply. They can erase something before they send it if they think it might be read the wrong way. They are much less likely to lose their cool over a text conversation. The people your kids communicate with can't see their faces over text, so they can't see their real-time emotional response, and if they call your kids out on something they texted, your kids can tell them they read it wrong. Conflict, a necessary part of a relationship, can be avoided over text.

Kids are losing the ability to take risks. They are losing the ability to figure out a way to fight boredom. They are losing the ability to creatively find ways to entertain themselves. Let me say that there are kids who are still creative and use their devices to create content instead of just consuming it; electronics and media aren't necessarily the problem. But the overuse of them might be.

Kids lose the opportunity to work their way through anxiety-producing situations when they can just retreat to their devices.

> They don't have to cope with sadness, anger, or frustration, either. They can escape reality by scrolling through social media or mindlessly playing games. Rather than learning from their pain, then, many kids instead become pros at distracting themselves from discomfort. Consequently, many lack confidence in their ability to step outside their comfort zones or deal with tough circumstances head-on.[3]

Avoiding uncomfortable emotions is something we all do. We all long to escape from anything that causes us pain, but pain is necessary in life and necessary for our kids. Pain teaches us what we need to change or things that we want to avoid in the future. Working through something that is painful builds endurance in our character. Pain can sometimes be a liar and tell us that we won't survive something, but when we make it through a painful experience and look back on it, we can almost always joyfully report that God really is enough and that he really does take care of us.

Comparisons

Although the Bible doesn't speak directly to social media, it does speak to the tendency in all of us to compare ourselves with others. It does speak to trying to find our identity in other people's good opinion of us. One of the first stories of the Bible speaks directly to this:

In the course of time Cain presented some of the land's produce as an offering to the LORD. And Abel also presented an offering—some of the firstborn of his flock and their fat portions. The LORD had regard for Abel and his offering, but he did not have regard for Cain and his offering. Cain was furious, and he looked despondent.

Then the LORD said to Cain, "Why are you furious? And why do you look despondent? If you do what is right, won't you be accepted? But if you do not do what is right, sin is crouching at the door. Its desire is for you, but you must rule over it."

Cain said to his brother Abel, "Let's go out to the field." And while they were in the field, Cain attacked his brother Abel and killed him (Genesis 4:3-8 CSB).

When Cain compared God's response to him with God's response to Abel, "Cain was furious, and he looked despondent." How often is that our response to something we see on social media? God comes back to Cain and basically says, "You do you. You do what is right. You will be accepted." But instead of finding any solace in that, Cain decides the best way to handle the situation is to kill what he determines is the source of his anger—his brother.

While our kids probably won't respond to jealousy or comparison with murder, Jesus says in Matthew 5:21-22 that if we call someone a "fool," we are guilty of murder. The Message puts it this way:

You're familiar with the command to the ancients, "Do not murder." I'm telling you that anyone who is so much as angry with a brother or sister is guilty of murder. Carelessly call a brother "idiot!" and you just might find yourself hauled into court. Thoughtlessly yell "stupid!" at a sister and you are on the brink of hellfire. The simple moral fact is that words kill.

You may feel like this is a bit of an extreme approach to dealing with the anxiety in our kids. But that's the point. The point is that the law of the Lord—don't be angry with someone and don't let envy control you to the point that you think someone is stupid—should cause us to fall on the mercy of Christ. Because of Christ, we are free from comparison. We no longer have to feel left out or undervalued or less than. He brought us into his kingdom and made us his brothers and sisters so that now we are completely accepted by God in Christ.

This full message is what our kids should hear from us. The beautiful truth is, even when they fail and fall into jealousy or feel anxious, they can turn once again to see their heavenly Father running toward them with arms open and a smile on his face—all because Jesus earned us the right to be called sons and daughters. When our kids are not getting "likes" or comments on their posts, we can remind them that the God of the universe loves them fully and completely—and not just some filtered version of them. He loves the unfiltered version of them. The version where every flaw, even the ones we don't see, shows through. He doesn't love us because we are beautiful; he makes us beautiful because of his love. We can show them that there is only one love that truly satisfies. This will crush the idol of comparison, and it will ease the anxiety of feeling less than.

Dwelling on the Good Versus Ignoring the Bad

How do we teach our kids to deal with negative emotion—how do we even learn to do that ourselves? Philippians 4:1,6-9 (csb) has a good word for us and our kids:

> So then, my dearly loved and longed for brothers and sisters, my joy and crown, in this manner stand firm in the Lord, dear friends. Don't worry about anything, but in everything, through prayer and petition with

thanksgiving, present your requests to God. And the peace of God, which surpasses all understanding, will guard your hearts and minds in Christ Jesus. Finally brothers and sisters, whatever is true, whatever is honorable, whatever is just, whatever is pure, whatever is lovely, whatever is commendable—if there is any moral excellence and if there is anything praiseworthy—dwell on these things.

Start with the foundation that we are dearly loved and longed for. When your child feels something negative, tell them that they are loved. Truly loved.

How do we teach them to stand firm when life is difficult or when they feel anxious or lonely? Tell them that they have a God who cares about them. He wants them to talk to him. He is a God of peace. Remind them that he will guard their hearts and minds. Then encourage them to fix their mind on things that are beautiful—the good news of what Jesus has done for us. Paul doesn't tell us to ignore problems or negative emotions; he tells us to bring them to our Father:

> The peace that He has for you is beyond your understanding. It's better than you can possibly imagine, and it will guard you from falling into those dark depths of despair that worry and anxiety can dig in your heart. "Peace, be still," the Lord says to your agitated heart. "I'm the God who holds today and all your tomorrows. You can trust in My Fatherly care."[4]

Give your kids something better to think about. Something better to fill their minds. Something to combat the anxiety and the worry.

However you want to regulate your kids' screen time is up to you. If you think having some screen-free times is helpful, then by all means do it. If you think that your kid shouldn't have their own device, then by all means, do what is right in your heart. But understand that taking away a device or limiting screen time won't change a heart; only God can do that. So pray. Pray that your kids know they are deeply loved. Pray that they have the courage and strength to fight against what the world tells them is perfect. Pray that they see through the filters. Pray that they are enraptured by the good news. Because truly that is their only hope.

6

The Diminishing Sense of Safety

September 11, 2001—I am sure you remember it. That day that is engrained in every American's memory. I was asleep when the news broke—my mom called me and told me to turn on the television. I remember going to get my youngest first. He was less than a year old and ready to eat. My oldest boy was expecting to attend his first day of preschool. But I just sat, staring at the images, trying to make my brain comprehend the depth of the tragedy unfolding in front of me.

I remember wondering if preschool would be canceled and formulating a plan with my family about where we would go if something happened where we lived, in San Diego. We are a military town, and the threat of violence here is very real. Those hours sitting in front of the television turned into days, which turned into weeks. I remember seeing airplanes in the sky the days following and wondering if one of them would be used in another terror attack. I pondered that thought consistently for at least a year after the attacks, and I sometimes still let that consideration run wild in my imagination. The first time I boarded a flight after the attacks, I looked at every person boarding, wondering what they were capable of. On 9/11, America suffered the deadliest foreign attack on our soil, and it changed everything.

I am sure you can remember where you were and what you were doing when you heard the news about the Columbine shooting as well.

I was folding laundry. My first son was about six months old. I was nursing him as I watched the news and wondered what type of world I was bringing him into. This wasn't the first school shooting in America, but it received more media coverage than any that preceded it, and it was the first one I remember. Since that day, school shootings have become increasingly common.

CNN counted 23 school shootings in the first half of 2018.[1] In two of those school shootings, ten or more people were murdered. Ten kids were killed on May 18 at Santa Fe High School in Texas. Seventeen people were killed on February 14 at Marjory Stoneman Douglas High School in Parkland, Florida.

On November 5, 2017, in Sutherland Springs, 27 people were killed and 20 were injured when a man opened fire in a church. On October 1 of that same year in Las Vegas, Nevada, 59 people were killed and 441 were injured when a gunman opened fire into a crowd of concertgoers. On September 10, 2017, in Plano, Texas, a man opened fire on friends while watching a Cowboys football game; 9 people died. On and on the list goes. I am sure you can think of a mass shooting that shook you, or maybe you read that list and your eyes skipped ahead because it's just too much to understand. Your brain can't take in the enormity of that many lives lost.

Then we have the ongoing threat of terrorism. In 2017, 8 people were killed and 11 people were injured when a man ran a truck into pedestrians near the World Trade Center in New York City. And the year before, a man went into a nightclub in Orlando and killed 49 people. Both men claim ties to ISIS.

You are probably aware of all these acts of violence. I remember a time when this wasn't our ongoing reality, but our kids don't have that luxury. For most of them, a life of mass murders, terrorist attacks, and school shootings is all they know. They don't know a life where there isn't a possibility of being in a terrorist attack because you are at a concert. Previous generations have lived with real threats and even world wars, but this is different. The point of terrorism is for each of us to live in fear, to have to go through metal detectors when we go to a baseball game, to always wonder if today is the day something horrible will happen. Those with elevated levels of anxiety feel this in such a deep way that at times, it can be debilitating. For someone who under normal circumstances may feel some anxiety, the threat of personal harm may heighten that sense of danger and increase their anxiety to an unhealthy level.

We are in a time of information overload. Incidents that we may not have heard about previously are on a 24-hour news cycle. Both Fox News and MSNBC started in 1996, and that changed the game on how we get our news. They need content and will continually look for something to draw people in. This can feed our anxious thought that something bad is going to happen. It can also embolden the egomaniacs who are looking for attention by doing something horrible.

Not only do we have this continuous news cycle, but the terrorists themselves use the internet to spread their reach even further. They post videos of violent acts. They distribute their propaganda as far as the internet reaches. Their videos serve two purposes: to add to those who agree with their rhetoric and to instill fear in the rest of us.

Is All Fear Bad?

Fear isn't a bad thing. God gifted us with the emotion of fear so we might learn to be safe and keep out of dangerous situations. He gifted us with a mind that can anticipate danger and intuition that can sometimes warn us of things we should be careful of. As I have noted in previous chapters, fear is a physical reaction to the threat of perceived danger. Clearly, this can help us be safe.

I love hiking. Almost every morning, I hike a trail that's only four minutes from my house. Once I'm on the trail, I am alone. It just leads to more trails through hills, away from our neighborhood. I relish the solitude and the quiet while I am out on my morning walks. The sunrise, the way the shadows play with the surrounding mountains, the sounds the birds make when welcoming the day, the way my dog takes off running as soon as I let him off the leash...all these things bring me fresh happiness every single day.

Occasionally, I see other people on the trails. When I do, my senses heighten. I check to see if they are alone too. I check to see if they have an animal. I check their clothes to see if they are wearing exercise gear. I check to see if they are a man or a woman. I take in my situation completely, and sometimes I change the course of the way I am walking. This is a good thing. You need to be aware of your surroundings (especially if you're like me and can't outrun a turtle). I have seen enough distressing news articles, listened to enough (or maybe too many) true crime podcasts, and heard enough stories to know that walking by myself in a remote location could be dangerous. Fear isn't necessarily a bad thing in a situation like this.

Today, our problem is that concern for physical safety is a constant thought, not just something reserved for certain settings and situations. The climate is such that our kids can feel unsafe anywhere they are—in school, at a concert, walking down a crowded street...it really doesn't matter. The threat of being in a dangerous situation is a constant companion. To those who already are predisposed to the emotion of fear, this can become debilitating. The good gift that God has given us of being aware of perceived danger can become an obsession. The truth of the matter is we can't send our kids out the door to school every morning and be totally sure they will come home to us safely. As scary as that may be, it has always been a reality. How do we help our children fight their fears of physical harm when they walk out that door when we have our own fears at play as well?

The Uncertainty of the Future

The truth of the matter is we can't just say, "Everything will be fine. Don't worry. You will be okay." We don't know the future. James 4:14-15 is very clear about this: "Yet you do not know what tomorrow will bring. What is your life? For you are a mist that appears for a little time and then vanishes. Instead you ought to say, 'If the Lord wills, we will live and do this or that.'" Our life is brief. This is why James encourages us to use the phrase "if the Lord wills." It is to remind ourselves that every day, every breath is a gift; it isn't promised. The sage in Ecclesiastes warns us repeatedly that we don't know the future and we can't control it.

The early church was confronted with physical danger regularly. They were tortured for their faith. In Hebrews 10:32-34 we read about this hardship:

> But recall the former days when, after you were enlightened, you endured a hard struggle with sufferings, sometimes being publicly exposed to reproach and affliction, and sometimes being partners with those so treated. For you had compassion on those in prison, and you joyfully accepted the plundering of your property, since you knew that you yourselves had a better possession and an abiding one.

The Bible is honest about physical danger. I know this may not seem encouraging, but we must help our children be honest. Our hope doesn't lie in our own ability to keep ourselves or our kids safe. Our hope lies in God alone, always. We put it in the same place those early Christians did: "You knew that you yourselves had a better possession and an abiding one." So instead of just seeking to protect our kids, we should look to educate them. Show them that the danger is nothing new and the strength, wisdom, and love of our God trumps any fearful thought. We are not alone, and neither are our children. Show them that the manifestation of danger is proof of the fact that the world is broken and in desperate need of a Savior. Use these opportunities to talk to your kids instead of ignoring or glossing over these scary situations.

The Certainty of Our God

- "Say to those with fearful hearts, 'Be strong, and do not fear; your God will come, He will come with vengeance; with divine retribution He will come to save you'" (Isaiah 35:4 NIV).
- "Peace I leave with you; my peace I give you. I do not give to you as the world gives. Do not let your hearts be troubled and do not be afraid" (John 14:27 NIV).
- "Have I not commanded you? Be strong and courageous. Do not be frightened, and do not be dismayed, for the LORD your God is with you wherever you go" (Joshua 1:9).
- "Even though I walk through the valley of the shadow of death, I will fear no evil, for you are with me; your rod and your staff, they comfort me" (Psalm 23:4).
- "When anxiety was great within me, your consolation brought me joy" (Psalm 94:19 NIV).

How do these verses match up with the reality of the dangerous world we live in? We must remind our children that this world isn't all there is. Even in the most dangerous of situations, we have something better than life. Once the fear of losing your life is gone, you can live it the way it was meant to be lived. We don't have to be a slave to terrorists or school shooters.

King David was familiar with being in physical danger. He wrote about it all through the Psalms. He lamented when something terrible happened. He questioned God when the world seemed out of control. Lamenting and bringing your questions to God are not bad things; they are biblical. We should teach our children to grieve and lament but at the same time show them to do it with their faces toward God. What is beautiful about the Psalms is that even though David knew he was in real physical danger, his truth is found in Psalm 63:3: "Because your steadfast love is better than life, my lips will praise you." God's love is better than life. That was David's truth, and it's our truth too.

When I was a child and feared a situation, my mom would always ask me, "What is the worst thing that can happen?" She encouraged me to think about my fear and follow it to its worst possible conclusion. Even if the worst thing that could happen was death, that actually wasn't all that bad, because we were made for more than this life. Romans 8:38-39 reminds us of this:

> For I am sure that neither death nor life, nor angels nor rulers, nor things present nor things to come, nor powers, nor height nor depth, nor anything else in all creation, will be able to separate us from the love of God in Christ Jesus our Lord.

Even death doesn't separate us from God's love.

We can't promise our kids they will always be safe, but we can promise them that God is in control. That he is watching them. That he sees them. That he has planned out every single one of their days. That no matter what the day holds for them, he holds that day. Be honest with your children. Prepare them for the very real and dangerous world we live in, but remind them, like the writer of Hebrews reminded those early Christians, that we have a "better possession and an abiding one" (Hebrews 10:34).

Ultimately, remind them that even when they fear or even if they walk through their day fearful, if they believe, then God sees them as trusting him just as perfectly as Jesus trusted God with his life. Jesus begged that the cup of God's wrath would not be his to consume, but he also said with faith in God's love and goodness that he wanted only God's will to be done. Jesus understands what it is like to face physical danger, and he did it perfectly on every believer's behalf so that we can know that our ultimate fate lies not in the hands of man but in the hands of God. He has made a way for us to be safe forever. Psalm 118:6 proclaims, "The Lord is on my side; I will not fear. What can man do to me?" That is our ultimate statement. That is our ultimate hope.

What can man do if we have God for eternity? In life or in death, nothing separates us from his great love and care for us. Give your kids that safety vest. Arm them in that security. Let God's love be what we teach them to hold on to.

PART 2

How the Church
Contributes to
Your Teen's Anxiety

7

"Do Big Things for God"

In the past, the church has always proven to be intolerant of mental illness. I distinctly remember being taught that mental illness was due to a lack of faith or prayer or just not trying hard enough. As a result, "those with mental illness can feel left out, as if the church doesn't care. Or worse, they can feel mental illness is a sign of spiritual failure."[1] Thankfully, this attitude is starting to change due to pastors with large churches being open about mental illness in their own lives or in the lives of their family members. Lifeway did a study on the church's attitude toward mental illness and reported these findings:

- Only a quarter of churches (27 percent) have a plan to assist families affected by mental illness according to pastors. And only 21 percent of family members are aware of a plan in their church.
- Few churches (14 percent) have a counselor skilled in mental illness on staff, or train leaders how to recognize mental illness (13 percent) according to pastors.
- Two-thirds of pastors (68 percent) say their church maintains a list of local mental health resources for church members. But few families (28 percent) are aware those resources exist.

- Family members (65 percent) and those with mental illness (59 percent) want their church to talk openly about mental illness, so the topic will not be a taboo. But 66 percent of pastors speak to their church once a year or less on the subject.[2]

As you can plainly see, the church is just at the beginning of its journey to understand mental illness and to know how to help its congregants. Because of this disconnect, the church is many times not only ill-prepared to help those in its care but also intolerant of those who experience mental illness. Often, we try to fix mental problems with a Band-Aid verse, and we end up doing more harm than good.

In an online article, a girl named Ayana shares her church experience of trying to get help for panic attacks and suicidal thoughts:

> A devout Christian my entire life, I wondered if God was punishing me with my panic attacks. I didn't tell anyone what was happening except for a few middle school friends who were no more equipped to handle my panic than I was. My parents are pastors, and they've always been nuanced in their views of mental health, but I didn't receive proper treatment for a decade because I was so afraid to talk about it—the church had created such stigma around mental health that I couldn't admit what was going on...
>
> One of the most harmful things I internalized from the church was that my mental illness was my fault. I had so much internalized guilt about the fact that I hadn't been able to make things go away, and it often came from fellow Christians chiding me for not giving my anxiety to God, as some put it. "If someone was like, 'Oh yeah, I'm a diabetic,' you wouldn't say, 'Not if you have Jesus,'" [Robert] Vore [a writer who talks about the intersection of faith

and mental health] says. "We have tangible evidence of these things. With most mental health things, we don't." Mental illness is never your fault, and prayer alone is not a sustainable treatment option.[3]

In this chapter and the next, we will look at two ways the church is contributing to the rise of anxiety in teens. The church not only is contributing to the rise of anxiety but also is ill-equipped to deal with the rise of mental illness. Many churches create the problem and then shun and shame the kids who suffer.

First, we will look at how the message to "do big things for God" is making our teens feel insecure and small. Then we will look at how the "be a good Christian" mentality is bound to make anyone anxious.

Inspiring Leaders...or Are We?

I have a dear friend who was an intern at a local church. When I first met her, she seemed sold out for Christ. On every single level, she gave everything she had. She talked a lot about how much she loved her church and how she loved giving so much. She also acknowledged that they asked a lot of her, but she didn't mind because she wanted to give her all to Jesus.

I watched as the intense calling they placed on her started to take its toll. The desire to perform for and impress those in leadership led to anxiety and eventually bitterness because she could never do enough. After years of serving, she started questioning the tactics they used to "inspire" their leaders. She brought her concerns to the leadership, humbly asking if they were maybe trying to control people or make them work harder by holding God's approval over their heads. They predictably told her that she was being divisive and kicked her out of the internship. She was devastated. She found a church that preached the gospel of grace instead of the gospel of "do more."

Unfortunately, the effects of that church continue to influence her life. She constantly battles depression and anxiety. She believes she isn't doing enough for God. It has been years since she was in the church, but the indoctrination has had a lasting effect. She often can't get out of bed in the morning because of the overwhelming depression and anxiety she feels.

Be the Leader God Intended You to Be

Much like society seems convinced that "accomplishments are king," the church has indulged in a culture that puts pressure on our teens to "do big things" or "be the leader God intended you to be" or "show the world how great God is by being great yourself." Somehow the normalcy of just living an everyday life loving God and others is no longer enough. You must live every moment to the fullest. You must tell everyone about God. You can't waste one single opportunity, because if you do, you are letting God down. The church has taken society's message, sprinkled a little bit of God into it, and repacked it with a Bible verse under it.

There is a very popular church in my area that has a very large youth group. They have an online training course for anyone who wants to become a leader or a stand-out youth. Here are just a few quotes from that training course:

- "It is not enough to just show up and be committed. You must be the best leader anyone can be."
- "Faithfulness is fruitfulness. It isn't just loyalty. You must reproduce. When I give you 5 can you make 10? If God gives you one person can you turn that into 10?"
- "Leadership is everything."
- "Success is seen on a Sunday. Are you building the church?"
- "God is impressed by what he has not given you, and he has not given you faithfulness. Being faithful catches the attention of God. He says, 'There is someone I can use.'"

- "God looks every time you don't take a shopping cart back to the spot it belongs."
- "Everything I do is so that every day God says, 'I still choose him.'"
- "To be a leader, you have to make more money than what you need. God has not just called you to be blessed but to be a blessing. You have a responsibility to prosper."
- "A culture of faith is a culture of working hard, like it's all up to us."

Now, I could explain why each of these quotes is complete rubbish, but instead, I want to reveal the basic premise behind the quotes and explain why it is unbiblical and damaging to our youth.

Live a Quiet Life

We are crushing our kids with a theology of glory, a theology that says God is impressed with our big works, a theology that says God only pays attention to the flashy, the productive, those of us who are extra. The truth of the matter is that the Bible urges you to "make it your ambition to lead a quiet life" (1 Thessalonians 4:11 NIV). Chad Bird, in his must-read book *Your God Is Too Glorious: Finding God in the Most Unexpected Places*, offers this comment:

> In other words, make it your ambition not to let "awesome" define your life, dictate your relationships, weigh the importance of who you are, or guide you in discerning how and where God is found.
>
> To lead a quiet life doesn't mean that you lower your expectations as much as you lower your gaze. Instead of looking up to the next accomplishment, the next rung on the ladder, you look down at the daily life you live, the children God has given you, the spouse by your side,

your aging parents, your friends, the poor and needy—
all those "little things" you miss when you're looking up
to the "next big thing" in your life.[4]

God isn't impressed with us when we return a shopping cart back
to the proper place. God is impressed with the glorious work of his
Son on our behalf. And unbelievably, we are hidden in Christ, so that
when God looks at us, he sees the perfect life of Christ. If impressing
God were as simple as pushing a shopping cart a few feet, then why
would he need to send Jesus to be our Savior, Advocate, propitiation,
and righteousness?

What if the church's message to our youth was the same as Paul's
message to the church of Thessalonica? What if we told them it was
okay to live a quiet life? What if we told them that God didn't look
down on them every day in judgment? What if instead we told them
that God placed his love on them from the beginning of time, that
before they did anything great or anything horrible, he loved them
because he is love? What if instead of telling them that a culture of faith
meant living like it was all up to them, we told them it meant living like
they believe Jesus has already done the whole thing for us? What if we
told them the hard work of the Christian life was believing what God
says is true: that we are loved, that we are welcomed, that we are wholly
accepted. The message of the gospel is meant to calm every fear and
heal every wound, not to excite every worry and damage every psyche.

Become the Man or Woman
God Called You to Be

I am sure that every teenager who has spent time in a youth group
has heard this sentence at least once. Personally, I can remember many
times when I heard this message shouted, pleaded, and cajoled by the
person trying to get us to be anything other than what we were. Typically, the music was exactly right to make you want to cry, the lights

were dim, and everyone was in just the right mood to admit what a failure they were and how this time things would be different. This constant rededicating, recommitting, and redoubling of our efforts only worked for a couple of days before we were all back where we were before but with a little more self-hatred because we had failed yet again.

I was listening to a popular speaker talk about this very thing at a large youth conference. She quoted John 10:10: "The thief comes only to steal and kill and destroy. I came that they may have life and have it abundantly." Then she made this statement: "The battle is that you become the man or the woman that God has called you to be. If you do this, you will have abundant life; it will exceed all expectations, greater than you can imagine." Not only is this statement's vagueness unhelpful; the statement itself could be construed as unbiblical.

First, what does it mean to become a man or woman of God? If what the speaker means is to live a sexually pure life (that was the context of the talk), then no teenager, boy or girl, can ever become the man or woman of God they are supposed to be. Every single one of us is born sexually impure. We are turned in on ourselves for gratification, and even those teens who don't pursue sexual promiscuity often revel in their sexual self-righteousness, which is just as detestable a sin as being sexually immoral.

The speaker also promises that those who somehow meet this undefined goal will have "abundant life that will exceed all expectations [and be] greater than [they] can imagine." Again, we need to define what this means. We automatically believe that "abundant life" means that we will have no problems, we will enjoy a fulfilling life, we will never lack anything, and all our dreams will come true. This type of jargon gives the connotation that life will be easy and full of success, not full of struggle. Though this may not be what she meant, I listened to the whole talk, and that's the message I came away with. And that message is distinctly antigospel.

The true meaning of John 10:10 is that because of what Jesus has done, because he came as our shepherd, we will have life and it will be abundant because it will be eternal—everlasting life through faith in Jesus Christ, not through material goods or worldly success. That is, "abundant life" in John 10:10 refers to everlasting life. It's a reward for a work that he has already done for us. It isn't something we can earn. In these verses, Jesus tells us that he is our good shepherd, that he has us, that he will care for us. This verse isn't meant to be used to get us to be better, more extraordinary people; it is meant to let us rest in the accomplished work of Christ.

The truth is, the more we dwell on the finished work of Christ, the more we will transform into the humans that God intended us to be, people who are free to love because we have been loved so richly, who are free to live lives of anonymity because our whole identity is found in the proclamation that we are accepted. This is important not only for us to realize but also for us to share with our anxious teenagers. This is the hope we are all looking for. Have you ever told your teenager that they were wholly loved and accepted by God, not because of what they have done but because of who God is?

Anxiety comes when we think the quality of our life or the quality of God's love for us depends on how much we pursue becoming a man or woman of God. Anxiety comes when we believe that our life hangs in the balance and that we have to make sure we are fulfilling all the demands of God or his love will somehow pass us by.

Not Doing Big Things but Believing Big Things

The church has propagated a message from most youth ministries that demands that the youth involved "do big things for God." What our youth ministries need to be promoting is "Believe in the big thing God has done for us!" Gerhard Forde says this:

> The righteousness before God comes only by hearing and believing. God makes us who we are. Works

performed on the premise that one was going to become righteous (or a man or woman of God) thereby are not good to begin with. They defend us against the goodness of God. They are done not for the neighbor but for the glory of the self. Works that can be called good, however, flow from righteousness as from an overflowing vessel, not into it as an empty one waiting to be filled...

It is not like accomplishing but like dying and coming to life. It is not like earning something but more like falling in love. It is not the attainment of a long-sought goal, the arrival at the end of a process, but the beginning of something absolutely new, something never before heard of or entertained.[5]

We need to tell our kids that they need to die—die to reputation, die to self, die to a belief that they can somehow earn the love of God. Only then will they be resurrected by the goodness of his love, the power of his grace. Faith justifies. That's it. Faith makes us right with God. Faith is a gift from God. So we don't have to try to have enough faith; he gives us exactly what we need. The glorious, settling truth is that every anxious thought concerning our standing before God is settled and has been settled since the beginning of time.

When we free our kids from believing that their good works earn them something—whether that something is a good life or God's love—then they will be free to work as though nothing depends on them. They will be free to give all their lives. They won't feel like they must get it just right but instead will know that Jesus did it just right for them. This calms the anxious heart. This lifts the burden of debilitating worry from the kids who are aware that they can't pull it off. It also frees the kids who try to pull it off from killing themselves from the effort.

Martin Luther famously said, "The law says, 'do this,' and it is never done. Grace says, 'believe in this,' and everything is already done."[6]

Why are we so afraid to give this message to our kids? We've tried every form of moral manipulation. Let's try the straight gospel and watch our children come to life.

8

"Be a Good Christian"

I grew up in a Christian home. Wait, let me rephrase that—I grew up in a super-Christian home. Everyone was a missionary or pastor or elder or deacon. Every time the church doors were open, we were there. My great-great-great-great-great-grandmother led Abraham Lincoln to the Lord. Actually, that isn't true at all, but I am sure if they had met, she would have convinced him of the truth that would set him free.

I learned early on that the way to earn approval and simultaneously keep everyone out of my real business was by being the good girl. I hate to brag, but I won "Miss Christian Character" in kindergarten. Surprisingly, I never won it again, but that is beside the point. By the time I was 14, I had already been on several short-term mission trips and spent a summer at an orphanage in Jamaica. I was *that* girl. The one who had a Bible verse stitched into her letterman's jacket. The one who always got up to share a testimony or give a word at youth group. The one who all the parents wanted their daughters to be like.

The insidious part of all of this was that I knew I wasn't a Christian. I knew I didn't believe. I didn't even care. But I did know all the right words and facial expressions to convince everyone of the exact opposite. Right after high school, I was a middle school youth leader, and on the outside, it looked as though I was clean as clean could be, but on the inside, I was a rotting corpse, as dead as dead could be. I took my charade all the way to Bible college. I just figured I could waste some time until I figured out what I wanted to do with my life. I also really loved to hear people say they thought I was amazing. I loved the praise of friends and family. But I didn't believe what the Bible said, and I just didn't care. I was content with my self-obsessed tomb. God had very different plans for me.

In college, we were required to attend prayer before our classes. I would regularly take a short nap or daydream during that time. But one day...well, one day, everything changed. As far as I was concerned, it was the same as any other day. I went into the chapel, found my favorite nap spot, and closed my eyes. But in that moment, God opened my eyes in the realest sense of the word. He came to me. I wasn't looking for him or for salvation or for forgiveness. I hadn't come to the end of myself. I was content in my role as the star actress. But God...God knew me. He saw me. He showed me that he saw me. He showed me that all my pretended goodness would never be good enough for him. He showed me that all my accolades from my family and church members were actually nothing before him. He showed me how desperately I needed something outside of myself to make me good.

So there, in the chapel I had pretended to pray in a thousand times, I prayed for the first time. He rescued me right out of the middle of all my nasty, dirty good intentions and bestowed on me a true goodness. God saved me in Bible college. My story is probably very similar to that of lots of kids raised in the church. I grew up thinking that the way to God was through my own goodness, but he came to me even though I was bent on badness.

Be a Good Christian

So far this book has primarily been about how society—the ones *over there*—have placed pressure on our kids to perform and how that has caused anxiety. But as we continue to turn our gaze inward, to our constructs, to our beliefs, I want to look at another way the church has contributed to the increase in anxiety among teens. I want you to think about the pressure you have felt in your own life when you have heard a sermon on how you need to be a better person. At first you may have felt inspired or felt a sense of urgency to work harder, but as the days wore on and you started slacking off in your newfound zeal, you started berating yourself for not doing better, which led to a feeling of anxiety that you aren't measuring up. Often that feeling leads to despair and wanting to give up altogether.

This is not an uncommon feeling. If all you are hearing from the pulpit or the books you read are rules and laws to do better, be a stronger Christian, or try harder, you will end up in one of two places.

One, you will feel pride because you think you are pulling it off. You will look at how good you've done and think that you are pretty darn amazing. You will look at others and wonder why they aren't pulling their weight. You will wonder why people can't just do what they are supposed to do, because you certainly are! But when you fail—and you will—you will feel anxious; you will feel like you have to make it up to God or he will be angry with you.

Or two, you will see that you can't do whatever it is you should be doing, and you will despair. You will look at others who seem to be strong, and you will think that God is happier with them. You will feel like a failure, like you just shouldn't try anymore. This also leads to a great sense of anxiety because you know you should be something you just aren't able to be.

Our kids are no different. They respond to the rules or laws in the exact same ways.

The church has got its message mixed up. We should not be focusing on what we need to do to be good Christians; we need to focus on who Jesus Christ is and what he has done to bring us into his family. Most serious teen ministries emphasize the wrong thing. While I believe they are well meaning, they are actually crushing kids instead of building them up. Calling someone to do the impossible work of being a "good" Christian doesn't help. The truth is we are unable to be "good" Christians—that is why Christ had to die for our sins and live the life that we couldn't live.

Unconditional Surrender

> The Lord is looking for a generation which is uncon-
> ditionally surrendered to Him—willing to obey and fol-
> low Him wherever He needs them to go. Because when
> we surrender to God without conditions, and obey Him
> without questions, His spirit will be unleashed without
> measure in such fashion only seen a few times since the
> New Testament church.[1]

This quote, from a very popular website for Christian teenagers, may seem solid at first glance. Let's stop and think about what it is asking of our teens. First it says that God is on the lookout for someone who will unconditionally surrender to and obey him. This command is absolutely impossible for anyone to live up to. Actually, let me rephrase that: Only one could live up to unconditional surrender, and he did it perfectly when he cried out in anguish, "Not my will but yours be done." No teenager, no human can live that call out. God was looking for someone to fulfill his law perfectly, and he found that in his Son.

The quote then goes on to say that if we surrender without condition and obey without question, God will then unleash his Spirit on us. But if God was waiting for us to get our acts together, to obey completely, to live sold-out lives for him in order to unleash his Spirit on us, the Holy Spirit would have never even ventured near humanity.

God doesn't unleash his Spirit on us because we have somehow earned it by our goodness; God unleashes his Spirit on us because our badness is so desperately wicked, he knew we needed something outside of us to turn our hearts toward him. We can't see that we are in need without the Spirit's help! God unleashes his Spirit not because we are good but because he is good, kind, and loving. The pressure that is placed on our teens when we tell them that it is up to them for God to move is not helpful—it is hurtful. The beauty of Christianity, the beauty of the gospel is that it's not all up to us, and if it was, we would never be able to have a relationship with God. He is perfect and demands perfection. The good news, the news that the church must communicate more clearly to our teens, is that Jesus supplied the perfection that God demands.

Just so you don't think this is some fringe website or blog, the book that this website is based on is currently at number one on Amazon in the category "Teen & Young Adult Christian Values & Virtues." While that is impressive, what is even more impressive is that the book was released ten years ago, and it is still the bestseller. I spent hours on the website and didn't see one reference to the forgiveness of sins or the fact that we are justified. This is dangerous ground.

Doubt Your Salvation

Unfortunately, this type of thinking isn't an anomaly in conservative Christian groups. I watched several different speakers at several different conferences, and they all had a similar message: "Be the best Christian you can be, and if you aren't, you probably aren't even a Christian to begin with." One speaker said, "The greatest heresy in the American evangelical and Protestant church is that if you pray and ask Jesus to come into your heart, he will definitely come in." There is a lot wrong with that statement, but the thing that would raise the levels of anxiety a young person would feel is that it makes them doubt that God has saved them. That sentence makes them believe that they somehow must do more than have faith in order for their salvation to be real. When assurance of salvation is gone, how could you have peace?

Our youth repeatedly hear that the path is narrow and they have to walk on that narrow path or they probably aren't saved. I understand that we want our teens to stay out of trouble. We don't want them to experiment sexually. We don't want them to try any illegal substances.

We want them to have good friends and make good decisions. But this sort of talk, this emphasis builds anxiety. The truth of the matter is most of our kids won't make good decisions. They will sin. They will make stupid mistakes. They will do dumb things. But the good news of the gospel is that even when they do those things, the Father still runs toward them with arms wide open. This will allay their fears and turn their worries into happiness.

Bear Fruit...or Else

How many times have you heard that true Christians display the fruit of the Spirit, so you better work harder at those fruit? That you should be patient, be kind, be gentle? The sermons I have heard that resemble that sentiment are countless. Then pastors take it a step further and relate specific ways you must bear fruit, ways people will see fruit in your life.

One such way is by dressing modestly: "If your clothing is a frame for your face, God is pleased. If your clothing is a frame for your body, you are dressing sensually, and God hates what you are doing." Again, there is a lot to say about this thought. On its face, it claims that if you just dress modestly, God is pleased with you. If that is true, then God must really be into the Muslim religion. He must be a big fan of the burqa. And he must absolutely hate every tribe that wears little to no clothing. He also must hate all the poor people who don't have the means to dress in anything but what is given to them; those dependent on others for their clothes are out.

Telling youth that God hates the way they dress will only inspire fear in their hearts. If this is the motivation for dressing modestly, then it will fade or fail or produce self-righteousness. Jesus had sterner words for the ones who dressed well than he did for the ones who dressed seductively to make a living. The church often seems to highlight a few "horrific" sins, and if you engage in one of those sins, you are a second-class Christian or not a Christian at all.

No mention of the sin of self-righteousness was included in this talk at all. The sins that got your name scratched off from the book of life included acting like the rest of the world, listening to what everyone in the world listens to, watching what everyone in the world watches, dressing like the rest of the world dresses. Again, Jesus's sternest words weren't for the ones who acted like the rest of the world; they were for the ones who acted how the religious community wanted them to, had their moral life down perfectly, and so thought they didn't need Jesus.

When the church tells our youth that their salvation is based on their ability to be a good Christian, it induces anxiety. Our kids will always wonder if they have done enough to measure up. They will question whether the sin they just committed somehow disqualifies them from the grace of God. They will constantly take inventory of their actions to see if they have enough good works to maintain a relationship with God. This is a shame, and it creates an insane amount of pressure and anxiety.

The End of Religion

Often what the church teaches its young people is not Christianity but rather religion. It is a tit-for-tat way of working their way into God's good graces. The truth is that the gospel of Jesus Christ puts an end to religion. It says "No more" to all our vain efforts of trying to earn our way into the family of God. Grace teaches us that we can't do it on our own; no amount of piety can merit the love of God.

Justin Holcomb affirms this in his exceptional booklet *On the Grace of God*:

> God loves you with gratuitous grace, the only kind there is. God's grace is unconditioned and unconditional. God is the one who loves in freedom. Unconditional love is a difficult concept to wrap your mind around. Many of us think (whether we admit it or not) there must be some breaking point where God gives up on us.

> Even if we successfully avoid believing this fallacy, oth-
> ers' overzealous cries still reach our ears: certainly, there
> must be some sin or amount of sin that is just too much.[2]

Our teens hear the "overzealous cries" of those who try to convince them that God's grace is somehow limited, that there is only a certain amount available to them, and then after that, they are on their own. God's grace is the exact opposite of limited. It reaches into depths that no one can fathom. It goes to the darkest places and shines the light of forgiveness. It reaches in the hiding place of the most corrupt to save them. That is the thought that calms the deepest fears. That is the thought that quiets all anxiety. No one is out of the reach of grace.

The world loves religion. The world loves someone who earns what they have. Our own hearts are infatuated with the idea that somehow, we are the ones who can be good enough to earn the love of a holy God. Robert Capon agrees:

> The world is by no means averse to religion. In fact, it
> is devoted to it with a passion. It will buy any recipe for
> salvation as long as that formula leaves the responsibil-
> ity for cooking up salvation firmly in human hands. The
> world is drowning in religion. It is lying full fathom forty
> in the cults of spiritual growth, physical health, psycho-
> logical self-improvement, and ethical probity—not to
> mention the religions of money, success, upward mobil-
> ity, sin prevention, and cooking without animal fats. But
> it is scared out of its wits by any mention of the grace
> that takes the world home gratis.[3]

The messages that I quoted earlier in this chapter are messages of "spiritual growth" and "upward mobility." What hearts need to hear are messages of grace to the downcast, the less than, the total and com-plete screw-ups.

Grace is most needed and best understood in the midst of sin, suffering, and brokenness. We live in a world of earning, deserving, and merit. And these result in judgement. "Condemnation comes by merit; salvation only by grace: condemnation is earned by man; salvation is given by God." That is why everyone wants and needs grace. Judgement kills. Only grace makes alive.[4]

Youth need to be made alive. They need to be told to lay their "deadly doing down"[5] and instead rest in the love of Christ for those who are anxiety ridden, those who can't quite seem to trust him enough, those who know they need to do better but can't seem to muster the self-control to change. We don't have to work for God's work. Jesus did that work. He did it perfectly. He did it completely. He did it on our behalf. We are now free to revel in that love, enjoy the benefits of what Christ has done. Our teens are free to reel in his love!

The church tries to control teens with a message of morality, but that never works. Sure, teens may be able to keep it together for a little while, but they will eventually become anxious or proud. Let's give teens the very message that Jesus gave his disciples:

> Come to me, all who labor and are heavy laden, and I will give you rest. Take my yoke upon you, and learn from me, for I am gentle and lowly in heart, and you will find rest for your souls. For my yoke is easy, and my burden is light (Matthew 11:28-30).

Eugene Peterson paraphrases it this way:

> Are you tired? Worn out? Burned out on religion? Come to me. Get away with me and you'll recover your life. I'll show you how to take a real rest. Walk with me and work with me—watch how I do it. Learn the unforced

rhythms of grace. I won't lay anything heavy or ill-fitting on you. Keep company with me and you'll learn to live freely and lightly.

In the church's effort to keep kids in line, it has been placing burdens on them. Burdens that they cannot bear the weight of. Burdens that make them anxious and worried. No teenager can live up to the perfect standards that God requires, but that doesn't mean God will push them away. Instead, it moved God to send a substitute who lived that perfect life that God requires and took the punishment that is deserved, which now allows us a life of rest. Religion breeds anxiety. Grace breeds rest.

Part 3

How You Contribute to Your Teen's Anxiety

9

Helicopter Parenting

One of my greatest pet peeves is the school drop-off and pickup lines. School drop-off and pickup should be a very easy process. It should go something like this: Your car waits in a line of cars. When the car reaches the drop-off point, the child (who should already have their stuff in hand) jumps out of the car and walks into the school. Sounds easy enough, right?

But what often happens is that when the parent stops the car, sometimes prematurely, they recite a speech they composed to their children about their undying love and approval of them.

Or maybe they decide their child is unqualified to get their backpack out of the car. I can't tell you how many times I have seen parents get out, go to the back of the car, and get the child their backpack because...I don't know why.

Or maybe they have an electric blender in their car, and a fresh smoothie is exactly what their kid needs to have a successful day at school. I am not sure what the thought process is, but these parents take an exceptionally long time to get their kids out of the car. My daughter always gives me a hard time about my lack of patience in the car line and tells me to recite the liturgy for road rage. Yes, there is an actual prayer called the Liturgy for Road Rage from the excellent book *Every Moment Holy*.[1]

The problem with the drop-off and pickup line is some parents can't let their children go—they need to give them some last-minute instructions or help them with their bags. These people are called "helicopter parents." According to the Oxford Dictionary, a helicopter parent is "a parent who takes an overprotective or excessive interest in the life of their child or children."

Always There for Them

In the *New York Times* bestseller *How to Raise an Adult: Break Free of the Overparenting Trap and Prepare Your Kid for Success*, Julie Lythcott-Haims takes an in-depth look at the problem of overparenting our kids:

> To fulfill our primary responsibilities as parents—keeping our kids safe and sound and making sure they get the right opportunities—according to our contemporary standards of safety and of opportunity, we parents have to run a lot of interference. All the time. And if we're fortunate enough to be middle or upper class, we have the time and money to be quite involved.
>
> With the ultimate goal in mind of our kids being successful in an increasingly competitive world, we bring a "no mistakes" mentality to our kids' childhoods, and we do our part by accompanying them and controlling as many outcomes as we can...
>
> We've created a role for ourselves, a position that's partly personal assistant and partly like the role high-end publicists play in the lives of some Hollywood stars: observer, handler, and, often, go-between. We are a highly involved sometimes formidable third party in all interactions that involve our children and other adults, always *there*, present physically or by cell phone, hovering, acting as our kids' eyes and ears, poised to anticipate

problems, provide paperwork or materials, and intervene when questions need to be asked or answered. We don't trust systems or authorities. We don't trust our kids to be able to work out their own problems. Put simply, we don't trust anyone.[2]

This lack of trust in our kids, others, and ultimately God has led to a serious problem in the way we parent. Functionally, we act as if we are the only ones who know how our children's lives should go, and we will make sure they run exactly as they should.

We attempt to prevent our children from ever experiencing pain, and if they do, we are there in a millisecond to fix it: "American parents seem to have equated 'good' or 'successful' parenting with ensuring our kids never experience even minor, short-term pain."[3] We think we must play the role of savior in their lives. We think we must make their lives as protected as possible. While we should protect, nurture, and love, we have taken it all way too far.

The Causes

In the early 1980s, a few events happened that changed the way we parent. First, we were introduced to "stranger danger," the threat of a stranger luring a child to a vehicle to kidnap. "Evidence suggests that the initial views of the 1983 movie *Adam*—about the 1981 abduction and murder of a child—was the catalyst for the fear of stranger abduction that is commonplace in America today."[4] I remember my parents giving my brothers and me a secret code word that was to be used if ever someone told us that they were there to pick us up from school (the word was "Castle Grayskull" from the much and rightly celebrated cartoon series *He-Man and the Masters of the Universe*).

The threat of stranger danger is overblown: "We *perceive* that our nation is a more dangerous place, yet the data show that the rates of child abduction are no higher, and by many measures are lower, than

ever before."[5] The truth is, kids are safer than ever, but we continue
to be more vigilant. We don't let our kids go anywhere by themselves
without checking in with them several times or digitally keeping tabs
on them.

Second, the 1980s saw the rise of the self-esteem movement and
the "participation trophy" mentality. We became unable to let our
kids feel the pain of losing a game or failing a science project, so everyone started winning: "American parents and teachers had been bom-
barded by claims that children's self-esteem needs to be protected from
competition (and reality) in order for them to succeed."[6] We don't let
our kids deal with the reality that they don't always win, even if they
try hard.

If we can't teach our kids how to handle failure, how will they
respond when they get passed over for a promotion? How do we instill
in them the need to work hard no matter the results when we teach
them that just showing up means they are a winner? We hinder our
kids' development as well-adjusted people when we don't allow them
to feel the pain of disappointment.

> The irony is that measures of self-esteem are poor pre-
> dictors of how content a person will be, especially if the
> self-esteem comes from constant accommodation and
> praise rather than earned accomplishment. According to
> Jean Twenge, research shows that much better predictors
> of life fulfillment and success are perseverance, resiliency,
> and reality-testing—qualities that people need so they
> can navigate the day-to-day.[7]

The Cost

We want everything to be good and comfortable for
our children. But that isn't the reality of the world we're

preparing them for. They don't learn to make choices or to construct possibility from the vacuum of boredom. They don't learn responsibility or accountability for their own behaviors. They don't get the chance to stumble or build resilience. They feel supremely accomplished for things they haven't really achieved on their own or, in the alternative, believe they are incapable of accomplishing things without us. And there's no buffer from the stress. There's no freedom. No play. Hell-bent on removing all risks of life and on catapulting them into the college with the right brand name, we've robbed our kids of the chance to construct and know their own *selves*. You might say we've mortgaged their childhood in exchange for the future we imagine for them—a debt that can never be repaid.[8]

It is no coincidence that anxiety and depression rates rose at the same time helicopter parenting became common. Kids don't know how to cope with stress because their parents have been handling every stressful situation for them their whole lives. When these overparented kids are young, typically they just go along with whatever the parent says, and they don't learn how to interact with others because the parents don't let them; thus they are cheated out of learning important life skills.

When overparented teens are in high school or college, they fall apart. They don't know how to work through something difficult because they have never had to before. Our kids become crippled by the fear of failure; they don't know how to decide for themselves because parents have been making all the decisions for them. This fear of failure leads to an anxious lifestyle, fretting over what to eat for breakfast, what class to take, and what type of car to get. Then when the teen becomes anxious from all the stress, they call their parents to get advice, and the cycle of reliance repeats. The only thing we have really taught them is to depend on us for everything. Why we love our kids relying on us is another problem I will discuss in the next chapter.

The *Journal of Child and Family Studies* did a study in 2013 of 297 college students. That study found that college-aged students who lived under helicopter parents were significantly more depressed and less satisfied with their lives.[9] As I have said before, depression and anxiety typically go together. Another study...

> looked at how helicopter parenting affects children with anxiety. Children and their parents were invited to a laboratory setting, where the children were encouraged to complete as many puzzles as they could in a 10-minute period. The puzzle tasks were designed to mimic the challenging and occasionally frustrating nature of homework and other academic tasks. Parents were permitted to help their children, but were not encouraged to do so.
>
> The parents of children with social anxiety touched the puzzles significantly more often than other parents. Though they were not critical or negative, they attempted to help even when their children did not seek help. This suggests that parents of socially anxious children may perceive challenges as more threatening than the child perceives them. Over time, this can erode a child's ability to succeed on their own, and potentially even increase anxiety.[10]

We must pause and ask ourselves if we are living as the parent who continues to touch the puzzle. Do you feel anxious when you don't touch the puzzle? Do you feel out of control when you can't do the work for your kid? Do you want your child to finish the puzzle so badly that you are willing to do the work for them? Are you afraid your child might not be able to finish the puzzle, and do you feel like a failure if they don't? Ultimately do you think that their or your worth is tied up in how successful they are at completing the puzzle? This identity piece causes us to do all sorts of crazy things, as we will see in the next chapter.

The Gospel Cure

Helicopter parenting is the result of believing you must be in control. It is the result of believing you know best. It is the result of believing you are the one who will protect your child from every evil they face. It is the result of not trusting God with your kids.

Now before you protest, let me say this again: I do believe we need to parent our kids. I do believe we need to protect our kids. I do believe we need to train our kids. But is your parenting and protecting getting in the way of their development? Are your parenting, protecting, and training accompanied by constant worry or excessive anger when your child makes a mistake? Do you freak out when they make a decision on their own or get a grade you don't approve of? Are you willing to cut corners or even do the work for them if it means they get a better grade? Do you push them athletically in ways that are unkind and obsessive?

If you aren't sure whether you are a helicopter parent, take some time to pray and ask God to reveal your heart. You could even ask your teenager what they think (*gasp!*). Promise them you won't argue with their answer.

Your relationship with your teen is supposed to change; they are growing and maturing (hopefully). I heard author, professor, and broadcaster Steve Brown say that as a parent he tried to say yes to his teens as much as possible. The goal of raising teenagers, he said, is for them to be making all their own decisions by the time they're 18. Try building a friendship with your kid. Step out of your role as decision maker and into that of advisor and trusted confidant.

If you are a helicopter parent, I have some really good news for you. First, you are forgiven for all the ways you try to control your children. Second, the Holy Spirit can give you the ability to change. You don't have to trust in your ability to control because we have a good God who is loving and wise and is in control of every situation. You can be free from the straitjacket of trying to keep it all together. God is with you.

Isaiah 41:10 is encouraging: "Fear not, for I am with you; be not dismayed, for I am your God; I will strengthen you, I will help you, I will uphold you with my righteous right hand." If you are a helicopter parent, you don't have to be afraid; you don't have to be dismayed. The Hebrew word translated "dismayed" means "to anxiously look about." You don't have to work to control the entirety of your child's life.

You also don't have to be ashamed you aren't the parent you should be. God claims you as his own, parenting failures and all. He is your God. He is God; you aren't. The weight that is on your shoulders doesn't have to be there. Only he is strong enough to control the world, so you can stop trying. He promises to give you the strength you need every single day to get through it. He promises to help you. He promises to uphold you.

So often, we parents think it is our job to give our kids the strength to get through the day. We think it is our job to help our kids get out of every problem. We think it is our job to uphold our kids. But again, we aren't God. We will fail when we try to do those things. Instead, let's lean back into him. Let's rest in the fact that the God who created the stars knows our children by name, and he has counted the hairs on their heads. He is very familiar with their struggles, and so he is the one who can help them, strengthen them, uphold them.

Instead of training a group of children to rely on their parents, let's train them to rely on God. Let's trust that God will help them even if they fail, even if there are terrible consequences to their failures. Let's show them that Jesus is close when something bad happens or when a tragedy comes into their lives. And let's ask for forgiveness for thinking we need to be Jesus for them. They have a Savior, and it isn't you. Point them to the one who never fails.

And then relax. Relax into his loving kindness for you. Relax into his upholding righteous right arm. He is for you. He is for your children. This will be a process for you. You will have to return to trusting God over and over again. But he will never tire of you returning. He will always be there running toward you with open arms. He will continually remind you that your performance or failures as a parent don't change his love for you. Nothing will separate you from the love that he has for you. So, dearly loved one, rest.

10

Using Our Kids Instead of Loving Them

Now the serpent was more crafty than any other beast of the field that the LORD God had made.

He said to the woman, "Did God actually say, 'You shall not eat of any tree in the garden'?" And the woman said to the serpent, "We may eat of the fruit of the trees in the garden, but God said, 'You shall not eat of the fruit of the tree that is in the midst of the garden, neither shall you touch it, lest you die.'" But the serpent said to the woman, "You will not surely die. For God knows that when you eat of it your eyes will be opened, and you will be like God, knowing good and evil." So when the woman saw that the tree was good for food, and that it was a delight to the eyes, and that the tree was to be desired to make one wise, she took of its fruit and ate, and she also gave some to her husband who was with her, and he ate. Then the eyes of both were opened, and they knew that they were naked. And they sewed fig leaves together and made themselves loincloths (Genesis 3:1-7).

I'm sure you're familiar with this passage, but if you skimmed it, I want you to reread it. It is important that you understand what happened in this story, because we repeat the same mistakes Adam and Eve made even today.

Adam and Eve were in paradise. There was no anxiety. There was no stress. There was no sickness. There was no sin. In Genesis 2:25, the Bible describes them as naked and unashamed.

But then the serpent, Eve, and Adam have a conversation in which the goodness of God is called into question. Adam and Eve decide to eat the food that God specifically asked them not to eat, and then "the eyes of both were opened, and they knew that they were naked." This is the state we now live in. We know that we are naked, and just like Adam and Eve, we are ashamed of our nakedness.

The very next thing they do is sew fig leaves together and try to cover themselves. And this, dear friend, is the exact same thing we are still doing today. We try to cover ourselves with our accomplishments. We try to cover ourselves with our kids' accomplishments. We sense that we are not as we should be. We sense that we need to cover ourselves. And so we go about the task of sewing fig leaves together with anything we think will take away our shame or our nakedness.

My son scores a touchdown—fig leaf. My daughter gets an A in a difficult class—fig leaf. My son becomes the student body president—fig leaf. My daughter looks especially pretty one morning—fig leaf. My son gets into an Ivy League college—fig leaf. My daughter performs flawlessly at her recital—fig leaf. My son plays guitar in the worship band at church—fig leaf. My daughter makes a fantastic play in softball—fig leaf. My son attends youth group regularly and is a leader—fig leaf. My daughter is a peer tutor for kids at her school—fig leaf. Each accomplishment that our kids achieve, we use to make ourselves feel better about how we are before God and others.

Maybe you don't do that. But let me ask you this: When your child performs poorly, or looks like a mess, or doesn't make the catch, or doesn't get an A, how do you feel? Are you angry? Are you depressed?

Does the strength of your emotion surprise you? Do you think that if you were a better parent, they would be a better kid? Check yourself next time you find yourself in a situation where your heart swells with pride or is dashed by disappointment because of something your kid has done. Ask yourself if you are using them as a fig leaf to feel okay about who you are or to cover your shame. The harsh truth of the matter is that you can't use your child to build your identity and love them at the same time.

Crushing Our Kids

First Thessalonians 5:11 says, "Therefore encourage one another and build one another up." We can easily see how this verse applies to our relationships with other believers, but do you ever think of how it applies to your relationship with your children? We are to build one another up.

When we look to our children to build our identities, we aren't building them up—we are crushing them. No human can bear the weight of that responsibility. One reason we place demands on our children to behave a certain way or to achieve a certain goal is that we like the way it makes us look. When we have good, successful, well-adjusted children, we feel like good, successful, well-adjusted parents. We are leaning on them to give us the identity that we believe we need.

Too often, we focus on what our kids can give us instead of what we can give them, let alone whether if we are giving for the right reasons. Even the most self-sacrificing parent might be so giving because they want their child to feel dependent on them (see chapter 7) or because they want their children or others in their community to think of them as good parents. So much of our identity is wrapped up in what people think of us, and since "parent" or "caregiver" is one of our main vocations, we put a lot of stock in how we look doing it. No wonder this crushes our kids. The pressure for them to perform so that we look good is paramount and completely destabilizing in their lives.

Our Okayness

Many of us find our okayness or our righteousness in our parenting. We find it in the way our kids turn out. This places an extraordinary amount of pressure on our children. If we are okay only when they perform well in all areas of their lives, they are bound to be anxious.

When my daughter was young, she fought (gave in to, really) a temptation to hit other kids when they crossed her will. I would like to say that each time this happened, the foremost emotions I felt were sorrow that God's law was not obeyed and concern for the other child's well-being. But honestly, the prevailing emotion was embarrassment at what other people must think of me as a parent. I was worried they thought that I didn't discipline, or that I disciplined too much, or that I didn't feed my kids organic, or that maybe my daughter had too many hormones in her milk. My main concern was myself. My main concern was whether I felt good about my parenting. I wish I could tell you that I no longer do this, that because my identity is grounded in Christ, I am more concerned about his holy law than I am about my reputation. The truth is, I still have to actively fight against the temptation to think that how my kids perform is my identity.

Author and speaker Rhonda Stoppe put it this way:

> When we raise our kids for what people think of us we are asking them to reflect our glory rather than God's. Maybe you don't think you're a glory stealer—I mean that phrase sounds rather harsh doesn't it? But if you tell your kids stuff like:
>
> "You represent our family out there, so don't blow it."
>
> "When you don't do your homework how do you think that makes me look to your teacher?"
>
> "Don't talk in church; what will people think?"
>
> In a way what you're saying to your kids is, "You've gotta measure up so I look good to my friends." When kids figure out that their obedience is how you measure

your success in the parenting Olympics, they're likely to resent and even rebel against your self-focused motivation.[1]

Our "glory stealing" not only makes our kids feel anxious but also turns them away from us. Why would they want to be around someone who is so obviously using them? Or maybe you have a kid who loves to perform, and they are happy to bear the weight of your identity...until one day, they do something wrong. Then what? Their whole identity is built on whether they please you. This mutual identity building is a detriment to you and to your child.

We try to make our kids do something that only Christ can do for us: We ask them to give our lives meaning. We ask them to make *us* feel like we are valuable because of *their* accomplishments. Jeannie Cunnion addresses this in her excellent book *Mom Set Free: Find Relief from the Pressure to Get It All Right*:

> Have you ever been tempted to attach your worth to your child's works? Have you ever been tempted to believe that your child's bad choices make you a "bad" mom and your child's good choices make you a "good" mom. Or maybe you've been more than just tempted. Maybe you've actually anchored *who you are* in *what your children do*. I certainly have.
>
> Now, listen. Of course it is good and right to be proud of the good choices our kids make and to be on our knees in prayer over the not-so-good choices our kids make. But if our *worth* is anchored to our child's choices, their good choices will inflate our heads and their bad choices will deflate out hearts. And that is just no way to live.
>
> More important, if our worth is anchored to our child's choices, we better believe they feel the weight of it. It's a pressure, a burden that they are not designed

to carry. It's too heavy. It will crush them. It *is* crushing them.[2]

If that quote resonated with you, I encourage you to go purchase that book. It isn't just for moms; it is for every parent who feels the pressure to make sure they look a certain way. There is freedom for you and for your kids. Freedom in the gospel. Freedom in your true identity.

Christ Our Life

Each of us is searching for love. We think we can get it by having a good family reputation or by having kids who seem smart, funny, or athletic. We think we can attain this by our own efforts, so we give it all we have. We try to be the perfect parent. We try to raise the perfect kids. All to attain this love. Friend, can I tell you the best news? You are already loved. The very thing you are looking for, you already have.

I wear glasses for distance, so when I drive, go to the movies, or attend church, I need to put my glasses on to see anything clearly. I cannot tell you how many times I have searched for my glasses, only to find I had perched them on my head so I wouldn't lose them. I have spent cumulative hours looking for what I already had. We do the same thing when we look to use our kids' accomplishments to make ourselves feel loved. The very thing we are looking for, we already have.

Whatever your role is in your teen's life—parent, grandparent, or caregiver—remember that *you are loved*. Truly, deeply, unalterably loved. I know this is a book about helping your teen who may be struggling with anxiety, but allow me to take a few moments to show you how loved you are. And please don't skip this. Most teens who struggle with anxiety have parents who do as well. So take this break and relax into what the Bible says about who you are and how you are loved:

- "Great is your steadfast love toward me; you have delivered my soul from the depths of Sheol...But you, O Lord, are a

God merciful and gracious, slow to anger and abounding in steadfast love and faithfulness" (Psalm 86:13,15).

- "The LORD your God is in your midst, a mighty one who will save; a mighty one who will save; he will rejoice over you with gladness; he will quiet you by his love; he will exult over you with loud singing" (Zephaniah 3:17).

- "Your steadfast love, O LORD, extends to the heavens, your faithfulness to the clouds...How precious is your steadfast love, O God! The children of mankind take refuge in the shadow of your wings" (Psalm 36:5,7).

- "See what kind of love the Father has given to us, that we should be called the children of God; and so we are...By this we know love, that he laid down his life for us" (1 John 3:1,16).

- "I have been crucified with Christ. It is no longer I who live, but Christ who lives in me. And the life I now live in the flesh I live by faith in the Son of God, who loved me and gave himself for me" (Galatians 2:20).

- "'The mountains may depart and the hills be removed, but my steadfast love shall not depart from you, and my covenant of peace shall not be removed,' says the LORD, who has compassion on you" (Isaiah 54:10).

- "I am sure that neither death nor life, nor angels nor rulers, nor things present nor things to come, nor powers, nor height nor depth, nor anything else in all creation, will be able to separate us from the love of God in Christ Jesus our Lord" (Romans 8:38-39).

You are loved. God doesn't just love you in a general sense. He loves you in a "the hairs on your head are numbered" sense. He loves you in a "rejoice over you with singing" sense. He loves you in a "nothing will be able to separate you" sense. He loves you specifically.

Your New Identity

At one time, your identity was found in your performance, and even now you may be tempted to find your identity in your kids' performance. That doesn't have to be the case anymore. Your new identity was given to you by your sweet Savior. Beloved, again, please don't skim over these verses. Stop. Read them. Read them again. Pray that the Holy Spirit will make them real to you, because the only cure for using your children to build your identity is seeing that you already have a better, lasting identity.

- "To all who did receive him, who believed in his name, he gave the right to become children of God" (John 1:12).
- "Welcome one another as Christ has welcomed you, for the glory of God" (Romans 15:7).
- "In him the whole fullness of deity dwells bodily, and you have been filled in him" (Colossians 2:9-10).
- "You are a chosen race, a royal priesthood, a holy nation, a people for his own possession, that you may proclaim the excellencies of him who called you out of darkness into his marvelous light. Once you were not a people, but now you are God's people; once you had not received mercy, but now you have received mercy" (1 Peter 2:9-10).
- "If anyone is in Christ, he is a new creation. The old has passed away; behold, the new has come" (2 Corinthians 5:17).
- "No longer do I call you servants, for the servant does not know what his master is doing; but I have called you friends, for all that I have heard from my Father I have made known to you" (John 15:15).
- "You did not receive the spirit of slavery to fall back into fear, but you have received the Spirit of adoption as sons, by whom we cry, 'Abba! Father!'" (Romans 8:15).
- "If the Son sets you free, you will be free indeed" (John 8:36).

- "In him we have redemption through his blood, the forgiveness of our trespasses, according to the riches of his grace, which he lavished upon us, in all wisdom and insight" (Ephesians 1:7-8).

You are a child of God. You are welcomed by Christ. You are filled by him. You are included in his people. You have received mercy. You are a new creation. You are his friend. You are adopted. You are free. You are redeemed. You are forgiven.

So whenever you feel anxious because your child has underperformed, whenever you feel like your world is spinning out of control because of something they have done, remember who you are. Remember whose you are. Come back to these verses and recall what God has done for you through the work of his Son.

Then share that with your kid. You tell them that there is good news for those of us who fail, there is welcome for those of us who don't have it all together, there is freedom for those of us who don't live up to our full potential. He has you, dear reader. He has your kids too. Rest. Trust. Repeat. And if you see that you have been using your child instead of loving them, it might be a good time to confess to them and seek forgiveness. Then rest. Trust. Repeat.

11

Can We Be Best Friends?

You know the story: A parent decides to throw a party for their teenage kid. They permit alcohol at the party because they will be there to make sure nothing goes wrong. Inevitably, the party gets out of hand, the police are called, arrests are made. The parent gets the blame—and rightfully so, because they allowed the party and the underage drinking.

The incident makes the news, and other parents react in horror: "I would never!" Or understanding: "Teens are going to drink anyway. At least an adult was present." Or indifference: "What adults do with their kids on their own property is their business." The parent may try to defend themselves by saying, "I thought I could control it. I guess the kids just drank more than I realized. I was trying to have a fun party for my kid. What's wrong with that?" Most people in the community would say that the parent who threw the party was trying too hard to be cool and not trying hard enough to be a good parent.

The movie *Mean Girls* depicts this sort of "cool mom" thinking. One day after school, a foursome of high school girls goes to queen bee Regina's house. When they walk in, Regina's mom introduces herself to the new girl in the friend group and says, "If you need anything, don't be shy, okay? There are no rules in this house. I'm not like a regular mom. I'm a cool mom. Right, Regina?"

Regina looks straight at her mom and says, "Please stop talking."

The mom says, "Okay," and then goes to make an after-school snack for the girls. She then brings the snacks upstairs with a tray of drinks. The heroine of the story asks if there is alcohol in the drinks.

"Oh gosh, honey, no! What kind of a mother do you think I am? Why, do you want a little bit? Because if you are going to drink, I would rather have you do it in the house."

The scene is exaggerated and funny, and we laugh at the mom, but the truth is, a lot of parents think this way. And while this is an extreme example of trying to be the "cool" parent, I am sure most of us have also compromised our convictions at some point in order to avoid upsetting our children.

This would be more of a temptation to me than being a helicopter parent. I want to be the one all the kids have fun with and enjoy being around. If I am not careful, I can let the desire to be fun overtake my parenting decisions. Some people are controlled by fear, so they try to micromanage every single situation. Other people are controlled by wanting to be loved, so they try to make sure their kids are always happy with them. Neither of these approaches is helpful.

Your teenager doesn't need another friend in their life; they need a parent. You may think that being friends with your teen would decrease stress and anxiety, but the opposite is actually true. The lack of rules, boundaries, and authority makes teenagers more anxious.

> "Children want and need boundaries. They cannot ask questions about how far it is to go," said Barbara Harvey, executive director of Parents, Teachers and Advocates in Atlanta, which helps parents become better at parenting. "They depend on parents to set the parameters and keep them safe." When children don't have boundaries, they become stressed. And this is the reason why so many children are stressed: They have no real security at home, Harvey said.[1]

TMI

"When a child is a parent's best friend, there is often too much pressure placed on the child to know about—and to be overly involved in—adult situations."[2] Not only does it cause kids stress and anxiety to not have boundaries, but when you treat them as a best friend, they learn too much about your life. I am a firm believer in letting kids into as much of your life as is appropriate. Be honest about your struggles. Be honest about your weakness. Let them know you are desperate for Jesus. But don't overshare. They don't need to know about all your interpersonal drama. They don't need to know about every broken relationship or every hurt feeling. And they certainly don't need to give you advice on how to handle a situation.

My daughter loves to know what is going on in my life and wants to help me if I am sad or upset about something. Her love is a help, but I must be careful not to tell her too much. Even though she is 15 going on 25 and incredibly mature for her age, I have to remember that her brain is not even completely formed yet and that she doesn't have the emotional or mental maturity to deal with my problems.

This is especially true if you are discussing your marriage or extended family problems with your children. When you talk about these relationships, you are sharing only your side of the story and also may not remember to update your kids when the relationship has been restored and forgiveness has been granted. They don't need to know—nor can they understand—the complexities of these relationships.

> For example, when researchers interviewed the adolescent daughters of divorce, they found that girls were more likely to experience psychological distress if their moms made detailed disclosures to them about their financial worries, employment hassles, personal problems, and negative feelings about their ex-husbands.[3]

True, Lasting Friendship

Is the answer just to be an authority figure in your teen's life and not even try to enter into a friendship? Of course not. I believe we can attempt to build appropriate, lasting friendships with our children. You should be there for your kids as a confidant and as one they want to run to when they are experiencing anxiety. Part of building this type of relationship with your kids is cultivating an atmosphere of grace in your home. This comes from understanding and believing who you are before God and what he has done for you.

As Tim Keller puts it, "We are more sinful and flawed in ourselves than we ever dared believe, yet at the same time we are more loved and accepted in Jesus Christ than we ever dared hope."[4] Accepting that sentence as truth will inform all your interactions with your children. It will combat self-righteousness, fear, anxiety, and anger. The gospel really does change everything.

A healthy friendship with your kids also comes from believing that you don't have to be everything for your teens and God is the only answer to their relational needs. You must relinquish to him the control you think you have. Pray that God brings other trustworthy adults into your child's life so that they can get good advice. Encourage your kids to look to youth leaders in your church or teachers from school to get help if they are confused or need to talk to someone. God can and will use other relationships besides you to encourage them in their faith and show them that they are loved.

Perhaps your relationship with your teen is nothing like a friendship. Remember, the Lord is close. He sees the brokenness in your relationship and in your heart. The Bible promises that our God "is near to the brokenhearted and saves the crushed in spirit" (Psalm 34:18). Don't think for a moment that he is indifferent to your suffering. He isn't. He understands what it is like to have close relationships severed. He is a "man of sorrows and acquainted with grief" (Isaiah 53:3).

The Proper Way to Love

How are we to love our children? How are we to help our relationship with them flourish and grow? We can look to Ephesians 4:24-32 to see the proper way to interact:

> Put on the new self, created after the likeness of God in true righteousness and holiness.
>
> Therefore, having put away falsehood, let each one of you speak the truth with his neighbor, for we are members one of another. Be angry and do not sin; do not let the sun go down on your anger, and give no opportunity to the devil. Let the thief no longer steal, but rather let him labor, doing honest work with his own hands, so that he may have something to share with anyone in need. Let no corrupting talk come out of your mouths, but only such as is good for building up, as fits the occasion, that it may give grace to those who hear. And do not grieve the Holy Spirit of God, by whom you were sealed for the day of redemption. Let all bitterness and wrath and anger and clamor and slander be put away from you, along with all malice. Be kind to one another, tenderhearted, forgiving one another, as God in Christ forgave you.

These verses aren't typically considered in the context of parenting, but they give great guidelines on how to treat people in your life.

The apostle Paul reminds us to put on our new self. Your true self is one who was "created after the likeness of God in true righteousness and holiness." You are an image bearer who has been made holy and righteous because of the work of God through Christ. If your child believes, they have the same status before God.

Because of our standing before God, we are told not to let the sun go down on our anger. I don't know about you, but I have gone to bed countless times while I was angry at my children. The beautiful truth is that even though that is true, I am still "created after the likeness of God in true righteousness and holiness." And reminding myself of my true identity drains the anger from my parenting. Anger in your life and in your relationship with your children will "give opportunity to the devil."

Paul provides clear instructions on how to relate to your child, build them up, and give them grace. Look for the ways God works in their life. Look for ways to encourage them. Try to encourage them about things that really do matter—not just "You had a great game," but rather "You have put in lots of hard work to improve at your position, and I want you to know I see that." Not just "I am glad you got a good grade," but rather "You must have studied for that test and been disciplined in order to get such a good grade on it." Don't just tell them that they are pretty or smart—look for specific ways to encourage them. You may have to work hard to see them in a new light and notice what they are doing.

If you have relationships with teenagers, you know you need the reminder to be kind, tenderhearted, and full of forgiveness. But the only way to maintain that posture toward them is to remember that "God in Christ forgave you." You are forgiven for every time you tried to win your child's affection instead of loving them in ways that may be uncomfortable. You are forgiven for all the times you were angry with them instead of kind. You are forgiven for not acting the way you should.

Share that forgiveness with your kids. You don't need to share every detail of your life, and you don't need to know every detail of theirs. But you do need to make sure you are living and loving in light of the way you have been extravagantly loved.

The best and healthiest way to be a friend to your teen is to point them to the one who is the best of friends. The one who cares more intimately, knows more deeply, and loves more faithfully than anyone else ever could. As you become more aware of his love, you will be able to share that relationship with them. And together you can cast all your anxieties on him because he cares for you (1 Peter 5:7).

PART 4

How Your Teen Gives In to Their Anxiety

12

The Desire to Be Successful, Well-Liked, and Good-Looking

As I mentioned earlier, my oldest son, Wesley, is enrolled at a local junior college and is playing football for their team. He has always been an offensive lineman but has never played center. This year the coaches asked him to learn that position.

(In case you aren't familiar with football, the center is the one who snaps the football to the quarterback. It is arguably one of the most underappreciated and yet important positions on the field. No one notices if you do your job right 100 times in a game, but if you do it wrong one time, everyone notices. If the ball goes over the quarterback's head or if it hits the ground, everyone knows you have screwed up. To learn this position in your sixth year of playing football is not easy.)

Wesley has always been more than capable at football. In high school, he was a team captain and won first-team all-league honors, so he is accustomed to being really good at his position. But this year has been different. He has struggled at playing center. He had eight bad snaps in his last game. His team won by a lot, but his performance left him feeling deeply discouraged. His coaches told him to "fix it," but we were all at a loss on how to do that.

About that time, I saw a picture of a Facebook friend snapping a football. I clicked over to his profile and saw that he had played 13 years in the NFL as a long snapper. I messaged him and asked if he would be willing to give my boy some tips on how to improve. He said yes and followed up with a conversation with my son. After the conversation, Wes came into my room glowing.

"Mom, that was incredible. The first thing he said to me was that I was more than a football player and that my identity isn't in how I perform on the field."

"Yes! That is so great!"

"Then he told me I don't have to try to be perfect out there."

"Exactly, babe."

"Then he talked about some things I could do to improve and said he would look at film of me snapping the ball to see if he could help with mechanics. Then the best part is he prayed for me."

"That is absolutely amazing. God really took care of you."

"Yep!"

This conversation blessed both of our souls. My Facebook friend told my son exactly what he needed to hear to ease his anxiety—and it can ease ours too. First, our identities are not in how we perform. Second, we don't have to be perfect; we can relax and do our job.

Here is the thing: The more anxious Wesley got about snapping the ball perfectly, the more he increased his chances of messing up. The more he messed up, the more he was down on himself for messing up. The more he was down on himself, the more pressure he put on himself. The more pressure he put on himself, the more he messed up.

The answer to breaking this vicious cycle is to remind our youth they are more than how they perform. Their identities are already secured in the work of Christ. If Wes, by the work of the Holy Spirit, can remember this, then he can go out and play football for fun, not to secure his righteousness. This is not just true for Wesley; it is true for every single one of our teens. It is what will help Wesley break out of the shackles of the pressure to perform, and it will help your teen break those same chains as well in any endeavor.

Teach Your Teen About Their True Identity

In chapter 10, we reviewed some verses about your true identity. Those verses are for your teenager as well. The freedom you felt when you read that you were loved, accepted, called, made holy, and forgiven is the freedom your teen needs as well. Their identity cannot be found in performance, even if that performance is being a "good Christian" or a "good kid." Their worth must be found in the fact that before the foundations of the world, God called them and set his love on them.

> Blessed be the God and Father of our Lord Jesus Christ, who has blessed us in Christ with every spiritual blessing in the heavenly places, even as he chose us in him before the foundation of the world that we should be holy and blameless before him. In love he predestined us for adoption to himself as sons through Jesus Christ, according to the purpose of his will, to the praise of his glorious grace, with which he has blessed us in the Beloved (Ephesians 1:3-6).

Our teens must hear from us that before they ever did anything wrong or right, they were chosen to be holy and blameless because of his great love for his kids.

Just as Wesley needed to hear that his identity isn't in football or how he performs on the field, your teen needs to hear you say the same thing to them. Anxiety comes from a host of different sources, as we have seen in this book, but one thing is for sure—it comes from misplaced trust. It comes from trusting in ourselves and in our actions to feel loved.

Living for the Approval of Self

Anxiety comes from the way we judge ourselves. Your teen's anxiety comes from a primal desire to believe they are a good person. You see this desire all over the Bible. You see it when Adam blames Eve for his sin. You see it when Eve blames the snake for her sin. You see it when Cain kills Abel because his offering wasn't accepted. You see it when King Saul looked for every excuse to explain away his sin. You see it in the Pharisees' attempts to justify themselves.

Each of us thinks back on the day and wants to conclude that we are indeed one of the good ones. We want to look out over humanity and be able to conclude, *Well, I'm better than most and not nearly as bad as some.* Our teens have this same desire. And when they do something stupid or you disagree with them, you will see that desire in full force. They will explain away their actions or make your rules seem foolish to avoid the anxious feeling that maybe they don't measure up.

The truth of the matter is that they don't measure up to God's standards, and neither do we. This is why trying to find peace in our own abilities or actions, whether hiking a football or acing a test, will never bring the solace we need. That comes only from a relationship with a good and gracious God who looks at all our shortcomings and says, "You don't measure up, but I have sent my Son to measure up on your behalf."

Living for the Approval of Others

A close relative of "living for your own approval" is "living for the approval of others." One of my favorite characters from the Bible was a stellar example of this. My guy, Peter, who couldn't stand up to a teenage girl because he was afraid. Peter, who years after that incident wouldn't eat with a certain group of people because he was living for the approval of a bunch of religious racists. Peter just couldn't get over trying to make the people around him happy even though it cost him his integrity. The more your teen looks for the approval of their peers, parents, teachers, youth leaders, and so on, the more anxiety they will feel. Living for approval is like running on a hamster's wheel—you just never get anywhere at all, and the work is endless.

As the commentator Matthew Henry said, "Those that

seek for glory and honor shall have them. Those that seek the vain glory and honor of this world often miss them, and are disappointed." Os Guinness wrote that we are to live our whole lives before what he calls the "Audience of One." When we do so we can say to the world, "I have only one audience. Before you I have nothing to prove, nothing to gain, nothing to lose." Living for an audience of one would simplify your life tremendously, wouldn't it? When God is your sole focus, decisions become so much easier. Your heart will know the peace and contentment that comes from seeking to please and glorify God alone. Your life will be richer because your pursuits will have eternal goals in mind, not earthly.[1]

While it may be easy to tell your kids to just live for the approval of God, it is entirely different for each of us to work out how to do so. The only way we can live for the approval of God without anxiety is to believe that he already approves of us because of Jesus's work on our behalf. So remind your teens of that. Remind them they don't need others' approval when they have the approval of the one who truly matters. Your teen can be free from the anxiety to approve of themselves, earn others' approval, and win the approval of God. And all this is because of the work of Christ.

That Day

Our teens may worry about the future. Will they get into a good college? Will they meet the right person? Will they make enough money? But we need to remind them of their true future.

Then I saw a new heaven and a new earth, for the first heaven and the first earth had passed away, and the sea was no more. And I saw the holy city, new Jerusalem, coming down out of heaven from God, prepared as a bride adorned for her husband. And I heard a loud voice from the throne saying, "Behold, the dwelling place of God is with man. He will dwell with them, and they will be his people, and God himself will be with them as their God. He will wipe away every tear from their eyes, and death shall be no more, neither shall there be mourning, nor crying, nor pain anymore, for the former things have passed away" (Revelation 21:1-4).

The next time your teen tells you they are worried or anxious about what is to come, remind them of those verses. Tell them that if God has eternity figured out, he can surely help with the next step. Remind them that a day will come when they won't ever feel anxious again. Tell them that even though they are forced to face anxiety now, a day is coming when that feeling will be a distant memory. Validate their feelings and give them hope for the future.

In their book *Unmapped*, Charlotte Getz and Stephanie Phillips pen this glorious paragraph about dealing with anxiety:

Drown, resuscitate, repeat. Fail, get forgiven, go again. Despair, hope, defeat, redemption, over and over, until one day you wake up and realize you're still anxious, but you see it more clearly for the cloudy lens it is, and you know—even though you're not there yet, because TODAY IS A DOOZY—you *know* that you're going to be okay. Ultimately, you will be whole. And you're headed there. So you breathe, and you put one foot in front of the other while recognizing that you're actually being carried.[2]

Your teen needs to know they are being carried. That Christ has gone through what they are feeling, and he feels it with them and loves them and sympathizes with them.

Hebrews 4 reminds us that Christ is our High Priest who sympathizes with us in our weaknesses. Anxiety may be a weakness that neither you nor your teen wants to live with, but Christ is right in it with you both. He encourages us to "draw near to the throne of grace, that we may receive mercy and find grace to help in time of need" (verse 16). Encourage your teen to run to the throne of grace. If they can't run, tell them to fall in the general direction of the throne of grace because Christ is moving toward them with open arms and a loving heart.

Responding to His Giving

In Matthew 6:25-34, Jesus speaks directly to all those who experience anxiety. Eugene Peterson paraphrases this passage so beautifully:

> If you decide for God, living a life of God-worship, it follows that you don't fuss about what's on the table at mealtimes or whether the clothes in your closet are in fashion. There is far more to your life than the food you put in your stomach, more to your outer appearance than the clothes you hang on your body. Look at the birds, free and unfettered, not tied down to a job description, careless in the care of God. And you count far more to him than birds.
>
> Has anyone by fussing in front of the mirror ever gotten taller by so much as an inch? All this time and money wasted on fashion—do you think it makes that much difference? Instead of looking at the fashions, walk out into the fields and look at the wildflowers. They never primp or shop, but have you ever seen color and design quite like it? The ten best-dressed men and women in the country look shabby alongside them.
>
> If God gives such attention to the appearance of wildflowers—most of which are never even seen—don't

you think he'll attend to you, take pride in you, do his best for you? What I'm trying to do here is to get you to relax, to not be so preoccupied with *getting*, so you can respond to God's *giving*. People who don't know God and the way he works fuss over these things, but you know both God and how he works. Steep your life in God-reality, God-initiative, God-provisions. Don't worry about missing out. You'll find all your everyday human concerns will be met.

Give your entire attention to what God is doing right now, and don't get worked up about what may or may not happen tomorrow. God will help you deal with whatever hard things come up when the time comes.

Respond to God's giving—that's how we can help our teens fight their anxiety. Help them see that they are being carried. Help them see what he has already given to them and done for them. You see Jesus cares deeply. Jesus cares intimately. He is so good to us that he gives us practical ways to fight anxiety that cost no money at all.

He tells us to look at a flower. He tells us to watch the birds. This mindfulness, being aware of our surroundings and what we are really seeing, is something that mental health professionals suggest all the time. He also knows how much we like looking in the mirror and tells us that staring at ourselves isn't going to change anything. How would it impact our or our teens' lives to just go outside and consider the flowers? How much could we learn from looking at the birds and seeing how our heavenly Father takes care of them?

The Holy Spirit must work in our teens' hearts to convince them of these truths. So as a parent, grandparent, guardian, or caregiver, simply share the gospel and pray that the Holy Spirit does his work. Then rest and trust that God loves your teen more than you ever could and that he will bring them along the path he has designed for them.

13

Conclusion

Anxiety in a man's heart weighs him down,
but a good word makes him glad.
Proverbs 12:25

As we have seen throughout this book, there are many factors to blame for the rise of anxiety among our teens. We have seen the ways that society has contributed to the problem. The desire to be accomplished in sports, academics, and social activism has pushed many teens into anxiety. The utter disdain for being normal has put teens in psychological peril. The way our teens must deal with a constant flow of information and navigating social media has also made its mark on their psyche. We have established the ways that the church is also culpable for adding to teen anxiety. The themes of being a "good Christian" and "doing big things for God" don't serve to help anxious teens but rather trouble them even further. Then we have explored the ways that we as parents, grandparents, caregivers, and guardians have unknowingly added to the problem. I asked you to take a hard look at yourself to see if you may be a helicopter parent, if you were using your child to build your identity, and finally, if you were trying harder to be a friend than a parent. Finally, in chapter 12, we looked at ways that teens' own desires increase their feelings of anxiety.

My hope is that in each chapter, you found a good word to make your heart glad instead of just the reasons anxiety weighs down the heart, as the verse above describes. My prayer throughout the writing of this book has been that teens and parents alike come to the realization that there is a good word to combat every fear. We have a God who asks us to cast all our anxieties on him because he cares for us (1 Peter 5:7). We should marvel at a God who cares for his creation in such an intimate and loving way. He doesn't demand that we get over our anxieties and trust him. As you work to help your teen remember who our God is, he reminds us that he cares for us and will never leave us or our children in this battle alone.

Below are a few snippets of devotional readings that have warmed my heart and encouraged me to trust in God's goodness during the tumult of helping others with anxiety or dealing with anxiety myself. May they encourage your heart while you encourage the heart of your teen.

> His *EYE* is ever upon us! His eye is a *Father's* eye, which is always quick, and always affects his heart. He has set his eyes upon us for *good*. His eye is *ever* over us—fixed immediately upon us.
>
> His *EAR* catches our every sigh, our every groan, our every desire! It is always open to our cry. He listens to us—as one most tenderly and deeply interested in us. He knows our every need—and he intends to supply us!
>
> Our heavenly Father has forever determined—that none of his children shall lack any *good* thing—and that he will not withhold any good thing from them.[1]

> Christ is kinder than the kindest. Could I gather together all the rays of kindness, pity, tender love, that have ever glowed in the heart...
>
> of a mother toward her child,
>
> of a bridegroom toward the bride,

of a brother to brother,

of a friend to friend—

all combined would be but as one tiny sunbeam, compared to that wondrous love which is in the heart of Christ for His redeemed people!

Nor is it less comforting for me, to remember that He who cares for me is changeless in His faithfulness and love.

Oh, the marvelous sympathy, gentleness, loving-kindness which Christ daily shows me, and which I know will never cease!

Hence it is a most reasonable thing for me to cast all my cares on Him. His presence, His kindness, His effectual power, His unswerving faithfulness—warrant me in leaving all in His hand. Oh, that I may ever have grace to flee to this refuge and hiding-place! Oh, that every burden, every fear, every foreboding, every jot and tittle of my daily anxieties, may all be entrusted to His loving hand![2]

In the midst of all the great rush of events and circumstances, in which we can see no order and no design—we well know that each believer in Christ, is as safe as any little child in the arms of the most loving mother!

Amid all life's trials and disappointments—our faith rests upon the character and the infinite goodness of God! We should have the faith of a little child—in a Father whose name is "Love" and whose power extends to every part of His universe! Here we find solid rock upon which to stand, and good reason for our lesson that we should never worry. Our Father is taking care of us![3]

I often think it requires more faith to go to Him with small things than in great trials. We are apt to think He will not take notice of our little difficulties, and feel ashamed to call upon so great and mighty a Being for every trifle. But this thought originates with the pride of our hearts, for in one sense the universe itself and ten thousand such worlds—are trifles to God.

But when we read that every hair of our head is numbered—what encouragement we have to take everything to Him who alone can deliver us out of all our troubles. I think carrying our little troubles and needs to God, honors Him even more than when we go to Him with greater.

O what a mercy to be persuaded that whatever may be our circumstances, God is with us, directing and overruling the whole for our good and for His own glory. To know that He is ours—and that we are His. To draw near in faith, telling Him all that is in our hearts, conscious of having the ear and heart of Jehovah toward us. Is not this true, substantial happiness?[4]

When we turn to the Bible, we find on every page the revelation—that God does care—and has personal interest in His people.

Christ assured His disciples, that the very hairs of their heads are all numbered; meaning that God personally cares for all the minutest affairs of our lives—He cares for us as individuals. His love is as personal and individual, as the love of a mother for each one of her children.

Paul took the love of Christ to himself—as if he were the only one Christ loved! "He loved me—and gave Himself up for me!" God's love is personal. He cares for us—for me!

Whatever your need, your trial, your perplexity, your struggle may be—you may be sure that God knows and cares—and that when you come to Him with it, He will take time amid all His infinite affairs, to help you—as if He had nothing else in all the world to do!

God cares! His love for each one of His children is so deep, so personal, so tender—that He has compassion on our every pain, every distress, every struggle. "As a father has compassion on his children, so the Lord has compassion on those who fear Him." Psalm 103:13. God is our Father, and His care is gentler than a human father's—as His love exceeds human love.[5]

My prayer is that as you have read this book, you have seen anxiety as complex and not just a "fix it and forget it" sort of problem. It isn't something to hide from and just pray it resolves itself. Stephanie Phillips shares how important this is:

> I had always thought of anxiety as a sin to counter or a weakness to be overcome, but now I was hearing it as a legitimate condition, and the exposure of this condition within myself was setting me free. *Un-shaming me.* There was a name for all the difficulty I battled on a moment-by-moment basis, and I was far from alone. The shame slowly ebbed.[6]

I hope I have equipped you to see the causes of anxiety, but I also hope you see that you can't solve it. Don't add shame to the anxiety your child is feeling. Don't put unneeded pressure on them to change. Just share with them what may be helpful and leave the change to the Holy Spirit. He is much better at it than you are. I promise.

We truly can trust and lean into our heavenly Father's care for us. I want to be very clear that even though that is true, we are not prohibited from using other means to overcome anxiety. In his inexhaustible grace and mercy, he has given us scientists who have invented medications to help decrease feelings of anxiety. He has given us doctors who have a desire to understand and help people who suffer from feelings of anxiety. He has given us professional counselors who long to sit and listen and advise those who feel anxious. He has given us pastors who have committed their lives to taking care of God's people. He has given us youth workers who look for ways to encourage our teens. All these gifts are here for us and our teens to obtain the help that is needed.

Please, don't just read this book and assume that now that you have some knowledge, you can solve your teen's problems. Look outside of yourself. This takes humility. Pray that the Holy Spirit will grant you the strength to admit you can't fix every problem. Pray for wisdom as you seek out a psychologist, therapist, or counselor. Be up-front with your pastor or other leaders from your church about what your family is going through. There is no need to pretend anxiety doesn't exist; it is detrimental to ignore it and hope it goes away. Drag it into the light where you can get help.

And please remember the good word. Remember the gospel, the good news that Jesus Christ lived the anxiety-free life that we are asked to live, and he also took the penalty for all the times we or our teens entertained anxiety as though it was a favorite houseguest. He did these things so that now we can stand in right relationship to God, know we are completely forgiven, and forever be assured of God's love for us. He did these things so that we can know our final home is with him, where every anxious thought will be a distant memory and where all we will know is joy and gladness forever.

Notes

Chapter 1: The Problem

1. Emily Tate, "Anxiety on the Rise," Inside Higher Ed, March 29, 2017, https://www.insidehighered.com/news/2017/03/29.anxiety-and-depression-are-primary-concerns-students-seeking-counseling-services.

2. Benoit Denizet-Lewis, "Why Are More American Teenagers Than Ever Suffering from Severe Anxiety?," *New York Times*, October 11, 2017, https://www.nytimes.com/2017/10/11/magazine/why-are-more-american-teenagers-than-ever-suffering-from-severe-anxiety.html.

3. Responses from a Reddit question posted in 2016: "[Serious] Psychiatrists/Psychologists of Reddit, What Is the Most Profound or Insightful Thing You Have Ever Heard from a Patient with a Mental Illness?," Reddit, https://www.reddit.com/r/AskReddit/comments/3ukp0f/serious_psychiatristspsychologists_of_reddit_what/?sort=top.

4. "What Is the Most Profound?"

5. Ron J. Steingard, "Mood Disorders and Teenage Girls," Child Mind Institute, https://childmind.org/article/mood-disorders-and-teenage-girls/.

6. American Psychiatric Association, *Diagnostic and Statistical Manual of Mental Disorders, Fifth Edition* (Arlington, VA: American Psychiatric Publishing, 2013), 189.

7. Denizet-Lewis, "Why Are More American Teenagers?"

8. *Diagnostic and Statistical Manual of Mental Disorders*, 189.

9. Although more white people are diagnosed with GAD, they may not be the ones who experience it the most; they may simply be more likely to receive proper medical attention, and it may be more culturally acceptable for them to admit being anxious.

10. Caroline Beaton, "Is Anxiety a White-People Thing?," *Tonic*, November 9, 2017, https://tonic.vice.com/en_us/article/mb35b8/is-anxiety-a-white-people-thing.

Chapter 2: Mental Illness or Elevated Anxiety?

1. Gabrielle Moss, "4 Ways to Tell the Difference between Stress and Anxiety," *Bustle*, January 18, 2016, https://www.bustle.com/articles/136328-4-ways-to-tell-the-difference-between-stress-anxiety.

2. "Anxiety Disorders," National Alliance on Mental Illness, https://www.nami.org/Learn-More/Mental-Health-Conditions/Anxiety-Disorders.

3. "Understanding Anxiety, Panic Disorders, and Agoraphobia," Anxiety and Depression Association of America, https://adaa.org/understanding-anxiety/panic-disorder-agoraphobia/symptoms.

Chapter 3: Accomplishments Are King

1. Jay Atkinson, "How Parents Are Ruining Youth Sports," *Boston Globe*, May 4, 2014, https://www.bostonglobe.com/magazine/2014/05/03/how-parents-are-ruining-youth-sports/vbRln8qYXkrrNFJcsuvNyM/story.html.

2. Used by permission.

3. Lyndsey Layton, "Study Says Standardized Testing Is Overwhelming Nation's Public Schools," *Washington Post*, October 24, 2015, https://www.washingtonpost.com/local/education/study-says-standardized-testing-is-overwhelming-nations-public-schools/2015/10/24/8a22092c-79ae-11e5-a958-d889faf561dc_story.html?noredirect=on&utm_term=.3584887de75e.

4. Frank Bruni, *Where You Go Is Not Who You'll Be* (New York: Grand Central Publishing, 2016), Kindle edition.

5. Kellie Bancalari, "Private College Tuition Is Rising Faster Than Inflation...Again," *USA Today*, June 9, 2017, http://college.usatoday.com/2017/06/09/private-college-tuition-is-rising-faster-than-inflation-again/.

6. "NCAA Recruiting Facts," NCAA, March 2018, https://www.ncaa.org/sites/default/files/Recruiting%20Fact%20Sheet%20WEB.pdf.

7. Michelle Singletary, "Get Real on Scholarships," *Washington Post*, March 12, 2011, https://www.washingtonpost.com/business/get-real-on-scholarships/2011/03/08/ABM4LfR_story.html?utm_term=.d4e5d8e28945.

Chapter 4: The Disdain of Being Normal

1. Hara Estroff Marano, "Pitfalls of Perfectionism," *Psychology Today*, March 1, 2008, https://www.psychologytoday.com/us/articles/200803/pitfalls-perfectionism.

2. Thomas Curran and Andrew P. Hill, "Perfectionism Is Increasing over Time: A Meta-Analysis of Birth Cohort Differences from 1989 to 2016," American Psychological Association, 2017, https://www.apa.org/pubs/journals/releases/bul-bul0000138.pdf.

3. David Brooks, *Bobos in Paradise* (New York: Simon & Schuster, 2000), Kindle edition.

4. Marano, "Pitfalls of Perfectionism."

5. Jenni Berrett, "You Aren't Lazy—You're Just Terrified: On Paralysis and Perfectionism," Ravishly, July 19, 2017, https://ravishly.com/you-arent-lazy-youre-just-terrified-paralysis-and-perfectionism-mental-health.

6. Sara Kelley, "Little Victories," OCD Stories, April 14, 2017, https://theocdstories.com/tag/perfectionism/.

7. Tish Harrison Warren, *Liturgy of the Ordinary* (Downers Grove, IL: InterVarsity, 2016), 22.

Chapter 5: Social Media, Electronics, and Our Kids

1. *The Common Sense Census: Media Use by Tweens and Teens,* Common Sense, 2015, https://www.commonsensemedia.org/sites/default/files/uploads/research/census_executivesummary.pdf.

2. Parul Sehgal, "An Ode to Envy," filmed June 2013 in New York, TED video, https://www.ted.com/talks/parul_sehgal_an_ode_to_envy#t-774793.

3. Amy Morin, "Why Technology Makes It Hard to Raise Mentally Strong Kids," *Psychology Today*, August 14, 2017, https://www.psychologytoday.com/us/blog/what-mentally-strong-people-dont-do/201708/why-technology-makes-it-hard-raise-mentally-strong.

4. Elyse Fitzpatrick, *Overcoming Fear, Worry, and Anxiety: Becoming a Woman of Faith and Confidence* (Eugene, OR: Harvest House, 2001), 120.

Chapter 6: The Diminishing Sense of Safety

1. Saeed Ahmad and Christina Walker, "There Has Been, on Average, 1 School Shooting Every Week This Year," CNN, May 25, 2018, https://www.cnn.com/2018/03/02/us/school-shootings-2018-list-trnd/index.html.

Chapter 7: "Do Big Things for God"

1. Bob Smietana, "Mental Illness Remains Taboo Topic for Many Pastors," LifeWay Research, September 22, 2014, https://lifewayresearch.com/2014/09/22/mental-illness-remains-taboo-topic-for-many-pastors/.

2. Smietana, "Mental Illness Remains Taboo Topic for Many Pastors."

3. Ayana Lage, "In Church, I Was Told My Mental Illness Didn't Exist. Here's How I Got Help," *Bustle*, March 2, 2018, https://www.bustle.com/p/in-church-i-was-told-my-mental-illness-didnt-exist-heres-how-i-got-help-8385140.

4. Chad Bird, *Your God Is Too Glorious* (Grand Rapids, MI: Baker Books, 2018), Kindle edition.

5. Gerhard O. Forde, *On Being a Theologian of the Cross* (Grand Rapids, MI: Eerdmans, 1997), 105-6.

6. Martin Luther, "The Heidelberg Disputation," thesis 26, http://bookofconcord.org/heidelberg.php.

Chapter 8: "Be a Good Christian"

1. Christopher Witmer, "Obeying God: Does Doing All This 'Christian' Stuff Really Matter?," theReb, April 2, 2014, https://www.therebelution.com/blog/2014/04/obey-god-does-doing-all-this-christian-stuff-really-matter/.

2. Justin Holcomb, *On the Grace of God* (Wheaton, IL: Crossway, 2013), 14.

3. Robert Farrar Capon, *The Astonished Heart: Reclaiming the Good News from the Lost-and-Found of Church History* (Grand Rapids, MI: Eerdmans, 1996), 105.

4. Holcomb, *On the Grace of God*, 13.

5. A line from the hymn text "It Is Finished," written by James Proctor in 1864.

Chapter 9: Helicopter Parenting

1. Douglas Kaine McKelvey, *Every Moment Holy* (Nashville: Rabbit Room Press, 2017).

2. Julie Lythcott-Haims, *How to Raise an Adult: Break Free of the Overparenting Trap and Prepare Your Kid for Success* (New York: St. Martin's Griffin, 2015), 43-44.

3. Lythcott-Haims, *How to Raise an Adult*, 26.

4. Lythcott-Haims, *How to Raise an Adult*, 15.

5. Lythcott-Haims, *How to Raise an Adult*, 15.

6. Amanda Ripley, *The Smartest Kids in the World: And How They Got That Way* (New York: Simon & Schuster, 2013), 109.

7. Lori Gottlieb, "How to Land Your Kids in Therapy," *Atlantic*, July/August 2011, https://www.theatlantic.com/magazine/archive/2011/07/how-to-land-your-kid -in-therapy/308555/.

8. Lythcott-Haims, *How to Raise an Adult*, 74.

9. H. Schriffin et al., "Helping or Hovering? The Effects of Helicopter Parenting on College Students' Well-Being," *Journal of Child and Family Studies* 23 (2014): 548-57.

10. Joel L. Young, "The Effects of Helicopter Parenting: How You Might Be Increasing Your Child's Anxiety," *Psychology Today*, January 25, 2017, https://www.psych ologytoday.com/us/blog/when-your-adult-child-breaks-your-heart/201701/the -effects-helicopter-parenting.

Chapter 10: Using Our Kids Instead of Loving Them

1. Rhonda Stoppe, "Is Over-Parenting Turning Your Kids Away from the Faith?," Crosswalk, September 4, 2018, https://www.crosswalk.com/family/parenting/teens/ is-over-parenting-turning-your-kids-away-from-faith.html.

2. Jeannie Cunnion, *Mom Set Free: Find Relief from the Pressure to Get It All Right* (New York: Howard Books, 2017), 169.

Chapter 11: Can We Be Best Friends?

1. Danielle Braff, "The Risk of Being Your Child's Best Friend and How to Draw the Line," *Chicago Tribune*, September 17, 2018, http://www.chicagotribune.com/ lifestyles/sc-fam-parent-child-best-friends-0320-story.html.

2. Braff, "The Risk of Being Your Child's Best Friend."

3. Gwen Dewar, "Should Parents Be Friends with Their Kids?," Parenting Science, 2013, https://www.parentingscience.com/parents-be-friends.html.

4. Timothy Keller, *The Meaning of Marriage: Facing the Complexities of Commitment with the Wisdom of God* (New York: Penguin Books, 2013), 44.

Chapter 12: The Desire to be Successful, Well-Liked, and Good-Looking

1. Elyse Fitzpatrick, *Overcoming Fear, Worry, and Anxiety: Becoming a Woman of Faith and Confidence* (Eugene, OR: Harvest House, 2001), 78. Internal quotes are from *Matthew Henry's Commentary on the Whole Bible* (Peabody, MA: Hendrickson, 1991); and Os Guinness, *The Call: Finding and Fulfilling the Central Purpose of Your Life* (Nashville: Word, 1998), 74.

2. Charlotte Getz and Stephanie Phillips, *Unmapped: The (Mostly) True Story of How Two Women Lost at Sea Found Their Way Home* (Charlottesville, VA: Mockingbird, 2018), 159-60.

Chapter 13: Conclusion

1. James Smith, "Comfort for the Christian," Grace Gems, https://gracegems.org/C/Comfort%20for%20the%20Christian.htm.

2. George Everard, "The Only Way to Obtain Relief under the Manifold Cares That Often Encompass Our Path," Grace Gems, https://www.gracegems.org/2015/11/cares.html.

3. J.R. Miller, "Our Father Is Taking Care of Us," Grace Gems, http://www.gracegems.org/08/04/worry.html.

4. Mary Winslow, "Carrying Our Little Troubles and Needs to God," Grace Gems, https://www.gracegems.org/2015/10/little.html.

5. J.R. Miller, "Does God Really Care for Us?," Grace Gems, http://www.gracegems.org/08/04/care.html.

6. Charlotte Getz and Stephanie Phillips, *Unmapped: The (Mostly) True Story of How Two Women Lost at Sea Found Their Way Home* (Charlottesville, VA: Mockingbird, 2018), 256.

To learn more about Harvest House books and
to read sample chapters, log on to our website:

www.harvesthousepublishers.com

HARVEST HOUSE PUBLISHERS
EUGENE, OREGON